The

Attitude

of

FAITH

Saying Yes to
God's Power in Your Life

FRANK DAMAZIO

**WHITAKER
HOUSE**

The Attitude of Faith:
Saying Yes to God's Power in Your Life

ISBN: 978-1-60374-114-9
Printed in the United States of America
© 2009 by Frank Damazio

Whitaker House
1030 Hunt Valley Circle
New Kensington, PA 15068
www.whitakerhouse.com

Library of Congress Cataloging-in-Publication Data

Damazio, Frank.
 The attitude of faith / by Frank Damazio.
  p. cm.
 Summary: "Through biblical teaching and personal examples, Damazio reveals that saying yes to God and acting with expectant faith can bring your largest dreams to fruition"—Provided by publisher.
 ISBN 978-1-60374-114-9 (trade pbk. : alk. paper) 1. Christian life. 2. Attitude (Psychology)—Religious aspects—Christianity. 3. Expectation (Psychology)—Religious aspects—Christianity. I. Title.
 BV4509.5.D23 2009
 248.4—dc22
                                         2009011953

As a pastor, teacher, and leader, Dr. Frank Damazio is a man of faith and vision. A "yes man" only to Jesus, Dr. Damazio is a contagious Christian who truly has a *yes* attitude. This book comes out of his own faith in God, which has caused him to say yes and amen to God's call on his life to go higher and see farther.

—Thomson K. Mathew, D.Min., Ed.D., Dean, *School of Theology and Missions, Oral Roberts University*, Tulsa, Oklahoma

Pastor Frank Damazio is known not only as one of the leading pastors in Portland, Oregon, but also as a friend and spiritual mentor to thousands throughout the world. His heart for the lost, his service to the community, and his concern for the gospel worldwide are an encouragement and blessing to many.

—Luis Palau, World Evangelist, *www.palau.org*

It is not difficult to recommend anything that Frank Damazio has written. When he puts his pen to the great themes of the Bible, you are practically guaranteed a spiritual feast of inspiring insights that encourage you to draw close to the Lord. I have always been challenged by Pastor Frank's unswerving trust in the compass of God's Word. In his forceful style, he guides the reader in a masterful presentation of the truths of God's Word on this essential subject. If you listen closely through the pages of this book, you will hear the overtones of joy that come through developing *The Attitude of Faith*.

—Mike Herron, Vice President, *Integrity Music*

Frank Damazio is a proven leader, a man of the Word, and a great gift to the church. His capacity to lead from a place of faith is inspiring, and his knowledge and relevant teachings on this subject of faith will be a great blessing to you.

—Brian Houston, Senior Pastor, *Hillsong Church*

In his latest book, Dr. Frank Damazio presents a positive message for how to live in today's complex world. While the message of most in their attempts to posit a solution in this troubled world is one of "No! No!" Frank gives the biblical message of "Yes! Yes!" found in 2 Corinthians 1:20. Damazio brings great ministry and leadership skills and writes with accuracy, clarity, spirituality, and focus. He has the professional training with a doctor of ministry degree and many years of experience as a pastor, missionary, educator, administrator, and church executive. I strongly recommend him and his new book to all who seek to live with a *yes* attitude.

—Kenneth Mayton, Ed.D., Assistant Dean for Doctoral Studies, *School of Theology and Missions, Oral Roberts University*, Tulsa, Oklahoma

Pastor Frank Damazio is a leader of leaders and a man of faith. He has brilliantly navigated one of the largest churches in America to a place where the congregation has a firm foundation in the Word of God *and* an expectation of the power of God to impact their daily lives. Most leaders prioritize either the truth of God's Word or the power of God. Pastor Frank has an extraordinary ability to bring both of these essentials to life. This book will encourage your faith to say yes.

—Randy Alward, President and CEO, *Maranatha! Music*

Pastor Frank is one of the most respected Christian leaders who not only writes great books but also lives the principles he teaches. This book is a must-read for every person—not only survive in these days, but also to achieve greater success in life. This success is not because of some motivational jargon, but because of the power of God that is in you. Read this book, say yes to God, and take action!

—Jimmy Oentoro, Chairman and Founder, *World Harvest*

One of the greatest messages I have ever heard Pastor Frank Damazio preach was delivered to our multisite congregation on the message of our faith attitude. It is a part of this book that is now in your hands, and I can say that it was one of the finest messages I have ever heard—one that had a powerful impact on our entire church. This book, proven on the testing grounds of life and ministry, will change your life for now and for eternity. I can't think of any subject more needed for twenty-first century believers than faith.

—Dr. Wendell E. Smith, Pastor, *The City Church of Seattle, Washington*

At many critical moments in my life as a Christian leader, God has spoken to me specifically through the pen of Dr. Frank Damazio. His books are biblical, practical, and relevant—with a strong prophetic edge that both mentors and equips the reader for the next level ahead. This is the case in his new book, *The Attitude of Faith*. Dr. Damazio gives us a book that is a balanced injection of biblical faith, and it is required reading for people who are determined to say yes to the will of God for their lives.

—Rev. Chris Hill, President, *The Hill Communications Group, Inc.*

This book is an especially important and necessary book for our times. In the midst of all the "doom and gloom," Christians can be affected and adopt a similar view as those who do not know the Lord as their Savior. This book helps to wake us up and remind us of what the Word says and declares. It will definitely encourage, motivate, and challenge you for the great things that God has destined for each of us.

—Rev. Dr. Rick Seaward, Senior Overseer, *Victory Family Centre*, Singapore

Frank Damazio's book *The Attitude of Faith* is insightful, clear, and challenging. It is filled with the revelation of how we can all live an everyday life of faith that releases God's purpose to us and through us. This book is about far more than just the theology of faith; it is about the foundational attitude that releases faith's potential.

—Paul de Jong, Senior Pastor, *Christian Life Centre*, Auckland, New Zealand

If anyone understands the power of faith unleashed through a *yes* attitude, it is Pastor Frank Damazio. From his leadership and discipleship materials to his life of positive expectation, the fruitfulness of his life and ministry flow from the belief that if we are willing to say yes to the will of God, it is God's will to bless us, and He will! This is a motivating, encouraging, and faith-building ladder to life filled with abundance and even surplus. Turn your no to a resounding yes, and watch as God reveals the great things He has in store for you!

—Tommy Barnett, Pastor, *Phoenix First Assembly*, *Phoenix Dream Center*, and Copastor, *The Los Angeles and New York Dream Centers*

Frank Damazio challenges every believer to put their faith into action, to have a *yes* spirit that responds in faith to God, and to see what God will do in and through them.

—Phil Pringle, Founder and Senior Minister, *Christian City Church*, Oxford Falls, Australia

Frank Damazio provides an in-depth study of the power that framed the universe—faith. Pastor Frank opens the door to the supernatural, which is available to every child of God. *The Attitude of Faith* provides the believer with practical application for possessing and exercising supernatural faith.

—Dennis Lindsay, President and CEO, *Christ for the Nations Institute*, Dallas, Texas

Dedication

This book is dedicated to the congregation of City Bible Church, a people who have an amazing level of passion and vision, a people who steadily raise the bar of expectation a little higher with every challenge encountered, a people who have responded to those challenges with a resounding, "Yes, God can. Yes, we believe. Yes to faith and no to doubt," a people who believe God is able to do exceedingly abundantly above all that we ask or think. Thank you, City Bible Church, for your attitude of faith!

Acknowledgments

I have never achieved anything of lasting significance in my life without the help of key people who have served and sacrificed with joy and focus. I would like to acknowledge...

- Cheryl Bolton, my longtime assistant, who aids my writing in every way possible.

- Jonathan Tennent of Whitaker House, for his editing and fine-tuning of this book.

- Christine Whitaker, who has encouraged me and kept this project on target as we worked with Whitaker.

- Bob Whitaker Sr., for his personal interest, phone calls, e-mails, and faith for this book. It would not have been written without his prodding and vision. Thank you, Bob!

Contents

Introduction

Unleashing the Power of *Yes*

But as God is faithful, our word to you was not Yes and No. For the Son of God, Jesus Christ, who was preached among you by us; by me, Silvanus, and Timothy; was not Yes and No, but in Him was Yes. For all the promises of God in Him are Yes, and in Him Amen, to the glory of God through us.
(2 Corinthians 1:18–20)

The *yes* attitude is a biblically correct attitude for living life. This attitude was the source of the apostle Paul's ability to serve God radically in an aggressive and dynamic life. It was the source of his endurance, ministry, and confidence. God's Word is faithful, and His message is absolute, certain, and guaranteed. God did not vacillate in His message or His plans; neither did the apostles or Christ's disciples, and neither should we.

The message they received was not "Yes and no," "No," or "Maybe." It was an absolute and definitive *"Yes!"* Final! Done! No doubts! No questions! The only proper response to God's "Yes" is "Amen," which means, "So be it!" It is a response that says, "Yes! God said it, I believe it, and I am building my life on it."

Second Corinthians 1:21 describes the attitude shaped by a *yes* conviction and perspective: *"He who establishes us with you in Christ and has anointed us is God."* This is the power that is unleashed in the *yes* person. Such people are established, confirmed, anointed, ready to be fruitful, and prepared to achieve God's will and plan.

Attitude is everything. All manifestations in the physical world began as ideas in the non-physical world. Everyone has a choice about how to think. If you choose a negative, wrong attitude, then you will create negative and wrong results. If you choose a positive, biblical *yes* attitude, you choose the attitude of faith, and you will see positive results.

Look for the end result you want to see and work backward. Imagine yourself surrounded by the conditions you desire to see, and, with a *yes* attitude, watch that vision become reality. The *yes* position or attitude is, "So be it. As You say, God, let it be." This attitude expresses affirmation and agreement with God, a positive confirmation and declaration of what you are believing and expecting.

Our yes is fixed in Christ and in His Word.

The *yes* word is a Bible word; it represents a biblical attitude. It is more than just positive thinking or mind over matter—it is an attitude that is founded in and on the Word of God and in the true God of Scripture. Our *yes* is fixed in Christ and in His Word. We are not just fantasizing or imagining whatever we want. We are saying yes to the God whom we believe *"is able to do exceedingly abundantly above all that we ask or think"* (Ephesians 3:20). We are bound to His character and to the boundary lines of Scripture. God will not give us things that are contrary to His character or that would harm or betray us as His workmanship.

A *yes* person unleashes the power of *yes* in his or her life by believing and standing on the Word of God. The *yes* person is an *amen* person with a heart that responds with a firm and sure stand on the absolute certainty and truth of what God has said. The *yes* person is one who is committed to living in agreement with God's Word in solemn acceptance and confirmation, declaring, "So be it!"

Take your *yes* position today. Start with a simple prayer of declaration:

Today, I take my *yes* position by faith. With a right attitude,
I give a resounding and definite "Yes!" to God, who will do

precisely what He has purposed—exceedingly, abundantly, and above all that I ask.

As you journey with me and unleash the power of *yes*, I believe that you will be changed in a very real and practical way. Your thinking will change. Your attitude will change. Your declarations and words will change, and your prayer life will change.

Chapter 1

Yes to Expectation

Two men walked through an empty field. One saw exactly what he expected to see—nothing. He waded through tall weeds toward a desolate orange grove, thinking, *What a useless wasteland!* The other man bounced over the weeds with excited expectancy. "This is it! This is the place! This is where my dreams come true! Can you see it? Over here is going to be a merry-go-round and over there I will put a roller coaster. This is what I have always wanted!"

The second man knew beyond the shadow of a doubt exactly what was going to happen with that empty field and its surrounding orange groves. He could not see it with his physical eyes, but he knew inside what it was going to look like, and he knew what it would take to make it happen. He could not see the dream; he could not touch it, but he lived with expectation for the day when it would become reality. It was a wild expectation that his friends laughed at, but today, that wild expectation is a multimillion-dollar theme park called Disneyland.

Nobody succeeds beyond his or her wildest expectations unless he or she has wild expectations. If Walt Disney had been willing to settle for a small dream, not only would Disneyland never have happened, but neither would have Walt Disney World in Florida, Disneyland Resort Paris in France, or Tokyo Disneyland in Japan.

Have Great Expectations

What are your expectations for your life? Do you have high expectations or low expectations? Or do you not have any and not

17

care? Are you excited about your future, or are you facing it with deep apprehension and perhaps with fear?

Say yes to expectation. Expectation determines what you will have in your life and future, but it also represents what you are willing to settle for. Are you going to settle for an empty field, or are you going to expect the fulfillment of the lifelong dream? Expectation is a very powerful force in your life, and you must learn how to cultivate it fully. If you believe that whatever you expect with faith and certainty will enter your life, then you will examine your expectation level and cultivate it to its highest potential.

> *Expectation is the power to have an idea that becomes so real that you see it and feel it before you can hold it.*

Expectation is the power to have an idea that becomes so real that you see it and feel it before you can hold it. It is like a giant magnet that attracts what you expect into your life. Expectation empowers you to think the unthinkable and do the undoable, and it turns uncertain hoping into certainty.

Everyone has expectations, and these expectations come in a variety of sizes. Some are huge, such as the dream job, the business you hope to create, the person you dream of sharing your life with, or the family you hope to raise. You may have expectations about how you will live life, about your health, about your happiness, or about your level of success.

Expectation can be defined simply as fixing your eyes on the promised blessing with an eager anticipation of its arrival. An expectation is a strong desire that is filled with anticipation and confidence about obtaining what is expected. To live with expectation is to live with hope, dreams, imagination, and desires.

Desire Is a Strong Feeling with an Intentional Aim

Desire is more than just wishful thinking. It is the passionate and resolute determination of the will to achieve that which is sought. When you desire something, you long for it and crave it. You have a passion for it, yearn after it, and strive to obtain it. A desire is a concentration of deep feelings, and it often implies strong intention and aim. It is not simply a bland wish but a desperate yearning that will give anything to obtain that which is desired. Desire is a longing for something that saturates the entire soul.

Psalm 20:4 encourages us, *"May He grant you according to your heart's desire, and fulfill all your purpose."* God can grant you your heart's desire. The thing you long for—that which you earnestly and passionately reach for—God can give to you.

The famous evangelist D. L. Moody reportedly spoke these powerful words of expectation to his sons from his death bed: "If God be your partner, make your plans large." God *is* our partner, and our plans can and should be large. Will you allow the Holy Spirit to open your eyes to see what God has in store for you?

Desire Is Focused in Christ

Psalm 37:4 says, *"Delight yourself also in the LORD, and He shall give you the desires of your heart."* Desire is a God-given purposefulness for your life that is first fulfilled when you surrender your life to Christ and allow Him to take control. When you surrender to Jesus, you belong to Him, and He has the keys to your life's fulfillment. As you allow Him to be the Lord of your life, and as you walk in obedience to Him, He will direct your path, focusing your desires into alignment with His will for your life. He will give you the strength and ability to see those desires become reality.

> *Calling the crowd to join his disciples, he said, "Anyone who intends to come with me has to let me lead. You're not in the driver's seat; I am. Don't run from suffering; embrace it. Follow me and I'll show you how. Self-help is no help at all. Self-sacrifice is the way, my way, to saving yourself, your true self."*
> (Mark 8:34–35 MSG)

The disciples made the decision to walk away from their own desires and to follow Christ's desires. We scarcely lack desire; we just focus it on the wrong things. Pure desire to follow Christ cannot be achieved until your desire for self is extinguished. Make a decision to focus your desire on loving and serving Christ; then, God will take your life and fill it with the desires that bring true success and true satisfaction.

> *Desire is anticipation that is founded in God, an attitude of the soul that believes in the greatness of God.*

Desire is anticipation that is founded in God, an attitude of the soul that believes in the greatness of God's will and in His work yet to be done. It is the cry of the soul as heard in Jeremiah 33:3: *"Call to Me, and I will answer you, and show you great and mighty things, which you do not know."* You cannot know God's desires until you know Him and He reveals them to you.

You have a choice. You can slumber and sleep your way through life, or you can wake up and live life to the maximum. Life is meant to be filled up with all the great things God seeks to do for you, in you, and through you. Expectation is best received and lived out as you align your total life to God and His Word, living with abandonment to His desires for you and setting yourself to be in agreement with God. Jeremiah 29:11 declares,

> *For I know the thoughts that I think toward you, says the LORD, thoughts of peace and not of evil, to give you a future and a hope.*

Expect Good Things from God

This is the part of your life I hope to help you change. I want to see you begin to grasp—or recover—real, heart-felt expectation. I want you to recover your will to desire. Without the power to desire something good, you will have great trouble nurturing expectation for your life.

Proverbs 10:24 says, *"The fear of the wicked will come upon him, and the desire of the righteous will be granted,"* and Proverbs 13:12 states, *"Hope deferred makes the heart sick, but when the desire comes, it is a tree of life."*

Hope by itself does not bring expectation. Desire by itself cannot bring expectation. It is the desire to see the promises fulfilled, fueled by faith in God, that brings a sense of expectation. The power to hope comes from a faith in God and a belief that He is good and that He will be good to you.

May the God of green hope fill you up with joy, fill you up with peace, so that your believing lives, filled with the life-giving energy of the Holy Spirit, will brim over with hope!
(Romans 15:13 MSG)

The Best Is Yet to Come

A story is commonly told about a terminally ill woman who had three months left to live. She was the last person you would expect to have hope, but hope is exactly what she had. She sat down with her pastor and discussed her own funeral arrangements—her favorite songs to be sung, the Scriptures to be read, the dress to be buried in, and finally, the most important part of the funeral arrangements: "When you place me in the casket, put a fork in my hand."

The pastor sat there, his mind racing as he tried to figure out how to respond. Was she beginning to lose her mind?

The woman smiled at him and explained, "When I was a little girl and we had guests for dinner, I always waited with bated breath at the end of the meal. Sometimes, my mother would simply clear the dishes, and the adults would sit around and talk. But sometimes, my mother would say, 'Keep your fork,' as she picked up the plates. Then, I would get excited, because I knew that the best part of the meal was coming. It could be my grandmother's deep-dish apple pie or my mother's velvet chocolate cake, but it was always the best part of the evening."

Her eyes glistened with joyful tears as she continued, "As my family and friends come to my funeral and see me lying in the casket with the fork in my hand, I want you to give them a message from me. Tell them that I said I'm keeping my fork because the best is yet to come."

As you read Romans 15:13 again, I want you to reach out and take hold of it in faith, knowing that the best is yet to come.

May the God of green hope fill you up with joy, fill you up with peace, so that your believing lives, filled with the life-giving energy of the Holy Spirit, will brim over with hope! (MSG)

What Are God's Thoughts toward You?

Before you read any further, think about that question. What are God's thoughts toward you? What does He think about you? What does He have planned for your life? What desires does He want to plant into your heart? What does He want you to expect?

Right expectation is rooted in God's thoughts, intentions, and purposes for your life.

You have been called to greatness. You must grasp how good God is and how great His thoughts are toward you. Right expectation is rooted in God's thoughts, intentions, and purposes for your life. In Isaiah 55:8–9, God tells you what His thoughts are toward you.

"For My thoughts are not your thoughts, nor are your ways My ways," says the LORD. "For as the heavens are higher than the earth, so are My ways higher than your ways, and My thoughts than your thoughts."

You have been called to walk through doors of opportunity that you have not yet seen. God said He has plans for your future, and they are good plans. Expect good things from God. Expect Him to open new doors for your life. As you travel on your personal Christian road, God will set doors of opportunity in front of you for your personal life, your family, your business, your relationships, and your church. In Revelation 3:8, Christ declared,

I know your works. See, I have set before you an open door, and no one can shut it; for you have a little strength, have kept My word, and have not denied My name.

Let me paraphrase this verse. "I have set before you an open door, and it will remain open until you are able to enter it. You will enter in sooner than you think, and when your moment of opportunity comes, your strength will not be wasted in efforts to make the conditions favorable. You will enter in at once because I have opened the door!"

Expect to open new doors of faith adventures that will necessitate getting out of your comfort zone, the area where you feel the most comfortable trusting God. Getting out of your comfort zone requires a leap of faith. When the door is open, move through it. Take a risk. Move into the unknown. To find bigger oceans, you must not be afraid to lose sight of the shore.

What doors might the Lord open for you if you *expect* some new doors? What doors have you ignored or fastened with a "No Entrance" sign, even though you could hear God saying, "Go through the door"? Expect new doors. Knock on doors of opportunity and keep knocking.

Keep on asking, and you will receive what you ask for. Keep on seeking, and you will find. Keep on knocking, and the door will be opened to you. (Matthew 7:7 NLT)

Personal Testimony

Mark and Jennifer,
Married Couple in Their Thirties

Since our courtship time, we knew that God would lead us to adopt. We decided that we would have three children and then adopt a fourth. After twelve years of marriage without children and the disappointments and heartbreaking effects of infertility, it seemed that our dream of a family would never happen. That is when the Lord told us in a very clear way that we should start the adoption process, so we did. In our quest for the rest of our family, we faced even more heartbreak.

While we waited, we even built a four-bedroom house to have room for our children, knowing for sure that they were coming. We didn't expect this new season of adoption to be even harder than infertility! We were to adopt twin baby boys, and we waited excitedly for their birth. The day they were born, the fifteen-year-old birth mother changed her mind, and our hopes were crushed. We knew all along that God wanted us to have children. We just didn't know when, who, or how, so we pressed on in what seemed to be an uphill battle, trusting and believing that the Lord was the one who would form our family.

After we had spent two years of looking for our children, God gave us a set of four—yes, four—siblings. They had been in foster care for two years, and we were chosen as their placement family. What a joyful day it was when we brought them home! A couple weeks after they arrived, we found out that one of the birth parents was trying to get our four-year-old back! After several months, he decided to relinquish all parental rights. We are now a family of six, with a house reverberating with noise and overflowing with love.

Expectation Requires Faith

Cultivate an optimistic faith outlook based on God's desires for you and His commitment to you. Psalm 37:23 promises, *"The steps of a good man are ordered by the LORD, and He delights in his way."* Tell yourself, "My steps are ordered by God Almighty. My life and future are in His hands. I expect good things to happen, and I declare the greatness of God to be released upon my life. The same God who has supported me in the past, who met the needs of those in Scripture, who faithfully takes care of other people today, can do the same thing for me."

Faith is an exceedingly hopeful perspective of confidence and trust.

> *Without faith it is impossible to please Him, for he who comes to God must believe that He is, and that He is a rewarder of those who diligently seek Him.* (Hebrews 11:6)

Expectation moves us to pray for great things from God. This is the attitude that is constantly diligent in fully expecting God to do the impossible. Remember: if God be your partner, make your plans large.

> *If God is your partner, make your plans large.*

How is your expectation right now, today, at this precise moment? How filled with faith and expectation are you about your future? Do you have a heart that throbs with deep feelings of hope and a great outlook on the future? Do you believe Psalm 16:6? *"The lines have fallen to me in pleasant places; yes, I have a good inheritance."* Do you believe Ephesians 3:20? *"Now to Him who is able to do exceedingly abundantly above all that we ask or think, according to the power that works in us...."*

The Enemies of Expectation

Natalie's dream was to become part of the Olympic swim team. She spent hours training and preparing, expecting to make the team. At age sixteen, she barely missed qualifying for the 2000 Sydney games but knew that she could make the 2004 games. But in 2001, she was hit by a car, crushing her left leg.

If you had known Natalie, which of the following two responses would you have given her? The first option is, "Don't give up. You can still expect to qualify for the Olympics. You still have a chance." The second is, "That's one dream that has died. Such a shame. She gave her whole life to one dream and then had that dream crushed in a few short seconds. What a waste! She will never know what she could have done if she had not had that accident. She will never reach her full potential or come close to realizing her dreams."

Expectation doesn't just drop into your lap without a fight. When you begin to look to the future with faith, when you begin to step through new doors of opportunity, there will be challenges and adversaries. In 1 Corinthians 16:9, Paul stated, *"A great and effective door has opened to me, and there are many adversaries."*

Natalie had many adversaries. Her first adversary was her physical limitations. She was a swimmer with only one leg. Her other adversaries were her own doubts, fears, and the negative words that others spoke to her, telling her that her dream was over. Her expectation should have been crushed with her leg, but it was not. She refused to give up. She continued working out, doing physical therapy, and eventually began to train again. In 2008, she qualified for and went to the Beijing Olympics.

Expectation is willing to take on the adversaries that lie in wait at the doors of new opportunity. In *The Message* Bible, 1 Corinthians 16:9 reads, *"A huge door of opportunity for good work has opened up here. There is also mushrooming opposition."* The *Amplified Bible* says it this way: *"A wide door of opportunity for effectual [service] has opened to me [there, a great and promising one], and [there are] many adversaries."*

The Hebrew word for *adversary* contains the idea of someone who fights against you and endeavors to shackle you and push you into a tight and cramped place where you have no way out. Your adversary hates you and is determined to defeat and overcome you. He is your enemy. What adversaries stand between you and your open door? What adversaries endeavor to bind and limit your opportunities? What is it that tries to defeat you and prevent you from seeing your expectations become realities?

1. The Enemy of Expectation Is Fear and Worry

Walter Chrysler, founder of Chrysler Motor Company, had a box sitting on his desk. Every time he worried about something, he would not deal with it then but would write it down and put it in the box to deal with the following week. When he opened the box later, he would find that most of the worries from the previous week had already resolved themselves without any ongoing concern or attention on his part.

The things you worry about must not be allowed to rob you of expecting great things from God.

The word *worry* can mean "to choke or strangle." The idea is to harass by tearing at or disturbing repeatedly. It is a nagging persistence that drains you of energy. The things you worry about and the fear you bring upon yourself must not be allowed to have power over your life or rob you of expecting great things from God.

What are the things that persistently whisper in the back of your mind? What are the nagging worries and fears that eat at you? Peter tells us, *"Give all your worries and cares to God, for he cares about you"* (1 Peter 5:7 NLT).

A farmer was sitting on his porch and looking at his fields when a friend stopped by to visit. Any conversation between two farmers inevitably comes around to their crops, so the friend asked, "How's your wheat?"

The farmer replied, "Ain't got none. Figured the weevils would get into the wheat and ruin me, so I didn't plant any."

The friend nodded his understanding and asked, "So, how about your corn?"

"Ain't got none," was the reply. "Didn't plant any because I was afraid the crows would eat it and ruin me."

"Well, what about your potatoes?"

"Ain't got none of them, neither. Was afraid to plant 'em because the 'tater bugs will get to 'em, and I'd be ruined."

By now, the friend was perplexed. "Well, what did you plant this year?"

"Nothing. I just played it safe."

Don't allow your worries to determine your future! If you play it safe, you will have nothing. So throw all your hopes and all your fears into God's hands and know that He cares about you.

2. The Enemy of Expectation Is Negativity

Expectation can be drowned easily in our lives by tragedy or disappointment. A sense of hopelessness or failure can kill the desire or ability to expect things to change. Deep inside, a voice whispers, "You want to be somebody, but it's not going to happen." In the inner place of your soul, deep in your heart, a war rages against expectation with thoughts such as, *You don't have a chance. It's just not going to happen. Life is against you, so give up. You can't recover from this.*

People like you should never have dreams like this. Why expect anything when you know you will be disappointed?

Proverbs 4:12 promises, *"When you walk, your steps will not be hindered, and when you run, you will not stumble."* Do not let pessimism hinder your steps from fulfilling your God-given expectations. Dread and fear feed a pessimistic attitude that seeks to make God smaller than your problems. Pessimism makes it easy for you to visualize a negative outcome for your life and then live in a way that fulfills that negative outcome.

Say no! This is not what God desires for your life. Make a concrete decision to remove the negative spirit, attitudes, and thoughts from your life. The mind-set that says, "God is not for me," is destructive and is an expectation killer. Do not allow yourself to become a doom and gloom forecaster of your own life. A negative outlook builds a wrong mind-set that dominates your thinking and results in a negative belief that your expectations cannot and will not come to pass. Compare the size of your problems to the greatness of God. The size of your God must grow!

Compare the size of your problems to the greatness of God.

3. The Enemy of Expectation Is Apathy

Another adversary of expectation is an apathetic mind-set that resists change and is content with the status quo. The attitude that thinks expectation costs too much thinks things like this: *It requires breaking habit patterns that are impossible to stop. It requires change—and maybe the cost won't be worth the reward. It is safer not to dream, not to hope, and not to expect good, because you will be disappointed. Instead, be satisfied with where you are today, and do not expect anything better for tomorrow.*

In the late nineteenth and early twentieth centuries, the primary crop in Alabama was cotton. As you traveled across the state, cotton fields stretched out as far as you could see. Then, in 1915, the boll weevil immigrated into Alabama from Mexico and began a rampage of destruction. By 1918, farmers were losing entire crops and going bankrupt.

A man named H. M. Sessions refused to give up and determined that the success of his small town depended on finding a new crop to plant. After research, he determined that peanut farming would restore the town's agricultural success. The problem was that the local farmers had planted cotton their entire lives, their fathers had planted nothing but cotton before them, and their grandfathers had planted cotton before their fathers. They did not want to take the risk and try something new. It took Sessions a year to find someone who was willing to buck the status quo and plant this brand-new crop. One year later, those who had followed Sessions had paid off their debts and were in the black. All of the other farmers quickly followed suit, and not only the town but the entire county was saved from bankruptcy.

All people have boll weevil times in their lives. Things are at a dead end, and the problems facing them are huge. It is easier simply to give up than to expect that something better is ahead. It is easier to keep doing what you are doing than to risk something new to discover God's best.

If you are in a boll weevil time, you must remember that you were created for more than this! God has a plan for your life, and it is a plan for a good future—a future of hope and fulfilled expectations. (See Jeremiah 29:11.) God promises that hope placed in Him is hope that will not bring disappointment. It is hope fulfilled.

> *God promises that hope placed in Him is hope that will not bring disappointment.*

Hope does not disappoint, because the love of God has been poured out in our hearts by the Holy Spirit who was given to us.
(Romans 5:5)

Abraham Overcame Discouragement

Be like Abraham. In Genesis 13, Lot had just turned his back on Abraham and walked away. Abraham had treated him like a son and had given him everything, and Lot had washed his hands of their relationship and walked out. Abraham could have given up.

He could have cried out to God, "Oh God, I'm so discouraged. My family has left me all alone in a strange country. I have nothing to show for it. Maybe I should just go back to Ur, where life was easier before You called me out here to this strange land." What did God tell Abraham during this time?

> *The LORD said to Abram, after Lot had separated from him: "Lift your eyes now and look from the place where you are; northward, southward, eastward, and westward; for all the land which you see I give to you and your descendants forever."*
> (Genesis 13:14–15)

Lift up your eyes and look out from the place where you are. Do not wait for things to look perfect before you begin to develop hope and expectation. Start now. Look from where you are right now. Look north, south, east, and west from right where you are, because that is the land that God is going to give you.

> *By faith Abraham, while he was being called, obeyed to go out into a place which he was about to be receiving as an inheritance, and he went out, not troubling his mind as to where he was going. By faith he lived as a foreigner without rights of citizenship in the land of the promise as in a land not his own, having settled down to live in tents with Isaac and Jacob, joint-heirs with him of the promise, the same one, for he was constantly waiting for and expecting the city having the foundations, the architect and builder of which is God.*
> (Hebrews 11:8–10 WUEST)

Abraham had an expectation that God was going to fulfill His promise and that the land was going to belong to him and his descendants. Hebrews says he was *"constantly waiting for and expecting"* the fulfillment of the promise. Abraham did not allow fear of the future, worry about the present, or regret about the failures of the past deter him from that attitude of faith and expectation in God.

Abraham knew that his chances of becoming a father were diminishing as he got older, but he persistently held to the promise

God had given him of being the father of many nations. Even though he had walked away from a land of comfort and ease, Abraham knew in faith that he would see the promise fulfilled. And Scripture never shows him looking back to the land of his forefathers. Instead, he always looked ahead for the city whose *"architect and builder...is God."*

Life is filled with expectation robbers—people and circumstances that seek to steal your expectations. Fear and anxiety grip people's minds with uncertainty and fear of what may happen, overshadowing hope. One of the great challenges of life is to lift yourself out of your current circumstances and rise up to the level that your expectation can take you.

Jabez Overcame Negativity

Jabez had an excellent reason to have low expectations. When his mother named him, she did not give him a name that indicated she had great hopes for his future. She named him for pain, sorrow, and affliction. (See 1 Chronicles 4:9.) He was not reminded of who he could be; instead, he was constantly reminded of the pain he had caused. Yet Jabez was not content to live within those low expectations.

> *Jabez called on the God of Israel saying, "Oh, that You would bless me indeed, and enlarge my territory, that Your hand would be with me, and that You would keep me from evil, that I may not cause pain!" So God granted him what he requested.*
> (1 Chronicles 4:10)

Jabez had large expectations that God could surpass the stigma placed on him by others. He believed that God would bless him and use him to be a blessing to others.

God's blessings for us are limited only by ourselves—not by His resources, power, or willingness to give. Refuse any obstacle, person, or opinion that restricts your expectations for your future. There are great, God-given opportunities before

God's blessings for us are limited only by ourselves—not by His resources, power, or willingness to give.

you, great open doors, and great rewards lying within your reach. Stretch. Expect. Believe. Persist. Possess.

The culture around you says, "Don't get your hopes up. You may be disappointed. Aim low and be safe." You have to break away from the autopilot of the masses that settles for the ordinary life, the no-hope life, the aim-low-and-be-happy life. This is not the expectation that God has for your life. Think of yourself as the pregnant mother who expects only the best from her pregnancy. With her imagination, she is able to live the result in magnificent detail until, eventually, the baby is born and she physically holds her "expectation" in her arms.

You do not need a high IQ, special skills, or an amazing education to raise your expectation. You simply must make a decision to partner with God and His Word and to believe what He says about you and your future. Lift your vision to match God's vision for your life. Decide. Expect. Change. Lift your vision and take the limitations off your life.

Ruth Overcame Apathy

When Naomi's husband and sons died, her two daughters-in-law were faced with a difficult choice. If they stayed in their homeland, they returned to the security of their families, but it was security with a limited future. They were widows, but they were widows with family who would care for them. If they chose to go with Naomi, they risked losing everything.

When Ruth chose to follow Naomi back to Israel, she walked away from a life of security into a life of the unknown. As a widow in a foreign land, she had no husband, no family, and no protector. There was no security for her future and no reason for her to expect anything other than an arduous and lonely life.

Ruth refused to give in to apathy and reluctance to change. She declared to Naomi, "*Your God will be my God*" (Ruth 1:16 NLT), and she walked into the unknown with the confident expectation that she had all she needed for a full life. In so doing, she walked into a future that extended past her present-day fulfillment of a life with a rich and good man, Boaz, and into the fulfillment of being the great-grandmother of the king of Israel and part of the lineage of Jesus.

Simeon Overcame Prolonged Waiting

Luke 2 tells the story of Simeon, who expected to see the Messiah before he died. He waited for years with an attitude of expectancy for the fulfillment of that promise. He did not give up, but he persevered in waiting, expecting, and knowing that God would fulfill His promise.

When he finally held the child Jesus in his arms, he said, *"Lord, now You are letting Your servant depart in peace, according to Your word; for my eyes have seen Your salvation"* (Luke 2:29–30). He had waited for years, faithfully coming to the temple, knowing that if God had told him this was going to happen, it was as good as done. There was no doubt, no questioning, no fear—only a simple faith that God would do all He had promised.

Don't Give Up

Abraham could have spent his life looking back at Ur of the Chaldeans in regret for what he had left. Ruth could have looked back to the life that she could have had in her home country. Simeon could have looked back at a long and happy life and been satisfied with settling for the blessings he had already received. But none of these people was content to settle. None was willing to give up his or her expectations. They set their faith in the God who does not change, who promises and fulfills every word. They set their hope on His words and lived lives of expectation, alert and waiting for the fulfillment of all that He had spoken.

Whatever your situation is today, whatever you fear in the future, whatever you regret from the past, lay them aside and fix your eyes on God. Set your hopes on Him. Place your faith in His Word. Focus your life and your desires on Him. The best is yet to come.

Prayer of Expectation

Lord, I believe that You are good and that You desire to release into my life wonderful, unimaginable, miraculous, great, and mighty things. Today, I pray with large expectations by the power of the Holy Spirit. Enlarge my vision. Increase my faith. Secure my future. Amen.

Chapter 2

Yes to Never Giving Up

Hanging in the U.S. National Gallery of Art in Washington, D.C., is a series of four paintings by Thomas Cole. The series is called *The Voyage of Life*. Each of the four paintings depicts a stage of life: childhood, youth, manhood, and old age. The first painting is *Childhood*. It shows a mountain with a dark cave at its base and a river flowing out of the cave. A beautiful timber boat glides out of the cave into a world of lush vegetation, flowers in bloom, and a peaceful, gentle surface on the water. Inside the boat is a laughing baby with a Guardian Spirit standing behind. The painting shows childhood as a time of wonder and joy.

The second painting is called *Youth*. The baby has grown into a teenage boy. He stands in the rear of the boat, confidently steering it toward a majestic white castle off in the distance. The riverbanks are still lush and green, and the Guardian Spirit stands on those banks, watching the young man boldly chart his course. The painting shows youth as a time of dreaming and confidence in which it seems like nothing can hold you back.

When we look at the third painting, *Manhood*, the scene has changed dramatically. The youth has become a man, the river has become a raging torrent, and the sky has become dark and threatening. The castle of dreams is nowhere to be seen, and the boat's rudder has broken. Ahead lie treacherous rocks with white water crashing all around them. The man in the boat is caught up by forces he can't control. With the rudder broken, he cannot steer his boat. All he can do is look up at the sky and pray. Meanwhile, the

Guardian Spirit sits hidden in the clouds. Cole is depicting adulthood as a time when the joy and wonder of childhood have been tamed by the difficult and tragic experiences of life, when the confidence and boldness of youth have been swept away by the harsh realities of life.

The final painting is called *Old Age*. The battered, weathered boat has finally reached the ocean. The dark clouds remain, but the water is still. The boat's occupant is now an old man, and his gaze is fixed firmly on the clouds out in front of him—clouds pierced by the glorious light of heaven, the light illuminating angels coming to and fro. For the first time in his life, the man sees the Guardian Spirit who has accompanied him on his journey. It comes, takes him by the hand, and prepares him for his journey into the heavens.[1]

You are on a journey called *life,* and you will face challenges and changes; some surprises you will like and some you will not. The green pastures may give way to a dark valley, and the gently flowing river may become a raging torrent. You may feel discouraged, lose perspective, and want to give up. The enemy of your soul will seek to steal your faith, destroy your hope, and take the *yes* spirit out of your life.

One of the most famous robberies in history is the Brinks Mat robbery of 1983. Six robbers broke into the Brinks Mat warehouse at Heathrow Airport in London and stole ten tons of gold, worth about forty-five million dollars. As great as this robbery was, it is dwarfed by a theft that happens every day in the lives of people in every city and country—the theft of hope. When hope and expectation are stolen, you lose something far more precious than gold and far more vital than money.

Romans 15:13 says, *"Now may the God of hope fill you...."* God comes to bring hope to you. Whatever your situation, whatever you are facing, He has His eyes on you and wants to invade your life with a powerful dose of expectation. He desires to fill you with anticipation, hope, and high expectation. In Jeremiah 33:3, God says, *"Call to Me, and I will answer you, and show you great and mighty things, which you do not know."*

God Calls You by Name

You are the one being addressed by name. God knows you. He knows your circumstances. He knows the secret thoughts in your mind that undermine your expectation. He knows the holes in your life where the hope drains from you. He knows you, and He has singled you out to touch your life. God is for you. In Psalm 91:3–5, God comes to you:

> *Surely He shall deliver you from the snare of the fowler and from the perilous pestilence. He shall cover you with His feathers, and under His wings you shall take refuge; His truth shall be your shield and buckler. You shall not be afraid of the terror by night, nor of the arrow that flies by day.*

God is concerned about you as an individual and has set His hand on you to deliver you, cover you, give refuge to you, and take fear from you.

God is concerned about you as an individual and has set His hand on you to deliver you, cover you, give refuge to you, and take fear from you.

God Has a Dream for Your Life

God has a plan for you, a word for you, a future for you. God has something great in store for you. You are not too old to believe and imagine. There have been people in their seventies, eighties, and even nineties who didn't allow their ages to limit their abilities to imagine and, as a result, brought about their greatest life accomplishments in their latter years. Have you already resigned from life? Do you think at fifty, sixty, or seventy that your life is over and there's not much left to do?

There's so much more ahead for you! There is so much more that God wants to do in you. There is so much more that He can do through you. But if you are already dead, just walk out the door and fall into a hole somewhere. If you're already dead and all we're waiting for is a funeral, then just go drop yourself into a hole and wait for someone to cover you up. But if you have breath in your lungs, God can use you. Say with Michelangelo, "Lord, grant that I may always desire more than I accomplish."

You whom I have taken from the ends of the earth, and called from its farthest regions, and said to you, "You are My servant, I have chosen you and have not cast you away: fear not, for I am with you; be not dismayed, for I am your God. I will strengthen you, yes, I will help you, I will uphold you with My righteous right hand." (Isaiah 41:9–10)

Notice what this great Scripture says about you. You are a servant of God. You have been chosen. You have not been cast away. God promises to stay with you, help you, and uphold you. Expect the best!

Expectation Prayer

Would you pause for just ten seconds and say this prayer?

Lord, I believe that You are good and that You desire to release into my life wonderful, unimaginable, miraculous, great, and mighty things. Today, I pray with large expectation by the power of the Holy Spirit. Enlarge my vision. Increase my faith. Secure my future! Amen.

Now, move into the future believing that God has put His hand on you for good. God will come to you and meet you where you are in life. He will visit you with a fresh expectation—right where you are. God comes to you with what you need, when you need it, and where you need it.

God Comes to Rekindle Your Fire

He puts poor people on their feet again; he rekindles burned-out lives with fresh hope, restoring dignity and respect to their lives—a place in the sun! (1 Samuel 2:8 MSG)

God speaks to you to revive your expectation and rekindle within you the fire of hope and anticipation. George Bernard Shaw said,

I want to be thoroughly used up when I die, for the harder I work, the more I live. I rejoice in life for its own sake. Life is no brief candle to me; it is a sort of splendid torch which I've got a hold of for the moment and I want to make it burn as brightly as possible before handing it on to future generations.[2]

Amy Carmichael, missionary to India, suffered many life disappointments and spent many years as an invalid, confined to her bed. Lying on a sickbed, she was still used of God to change the lives of many. The work she began continues to this day with a home to care for orphans and a hospital staffed by those who were raised in the orphanage. She wrote a poem called "Flame of God," and the last verse goes as follows.

> Give me the love that leads the way,
> The faith that nothing can dismay,
> The hope no disappointments tire,
> The passion that will burn like fire;
> Let me not sink to be a clod;
> Make me Thy fuel, Flame of God.[3]

God wants to rekindle a fire in your heart. If you are confined to a sickbed, He is with you. If you are trapped in a hopeless situation, He will bring hope to your heart. He will give you a fresh expectation for what He can do in and through you, starting right where you are. He has His hand on you, and He will use you where you are to do great things for Him.

God wants to rekindle a fire in your heart.

God Comes to Restore Your Strength

If your strength is drained and you have become depleted, exhausted, spent, and used up (see Psalm 32:4), God wants to come and give you fresh strength. He wants to speak fresh, new hope deep into your heart and restore your expectation.

Job 4:4 says, *"Your words have put stumbling people on their feet, put fresh hope in people about to collapse"* (MSG). If you have been drained of your hope for the future, this is a sign that God is moving toward you to take you by the hand and lift you up.

God Comes to You When You Have Been Worn Down

Job 14:7 promises, *"For a tree there is always hope. Chop it down and it still has a chance—its roots can put out fresh sprouts"* (MSG). Have the repeated blows of life's disappointments and failures chopped at your roots until you feel you have been cut down? Do you feel like you have been ground down to nothing by the grinding of life's ways? Do you feel like you are being gradually reduced down to a place of no hope?

If this is the case, don't give up! You are just the kind of person God has promised to lift up and fill with new hope. Grasp hold of the truth in Lamentations 3:20–24:

> *I remember it all—oh, how well I remember—the feeling of hitting the bottom. But there's one other thing I remember, and remembering, I keep a grip on hope: God's loyal love couldn't have run out, his merciful love couldn't have dried up. They're created new every morning. How great your faithfulness! I'm sticking with God (I say it over and over). He's all I've got left.*
>
> (MSG)

God Comes to Restore Expectation If You Have Quit

Are you one of those people who have stopped short of the goal? Have you stopped too soon? Are you like the woman who was told to gather the empty vessels for a supernatural supply of oil but stopped short?

> *Now it came to pass, when the vessels were full, that she said to her son, "Bring me another vessel." And he said to her, "There is not another vessel." So the oil ceased.* (2 Kings 4:6)

The woman had smaller expectations than God had supply! What would have happened if she had gathered more vessels? What would have happened if she had expected and prepared for more?

Are you like the king in 2 Kings 13:18 who was told to strike the ground with arrows as a sign of defeating the enemy but stopped short? He struck the ground only three times and then stopped. The prophet rebuked him for stopping short instead of persevering, and as a result, he achieved only a partial victory over the enemy.

God has a complete victory for you. He has an abundant miracle prepared for you. Do not settle for a partial victory. Do not stop short of what He has promised. Do not settle for a partial fulfillment of His Word, but keep moving forward to see all your expectations come to pass.

> *God has a complete victory for you. Do not stop short of what He has promised.*

Expectation for achievement is largely the product of steadily raising one's level of aspiration. Celebrate what you accomplish, but raise the bar a little higher each time you succeed. Don't quit too soon or stop short.

William Carey could have quit and no one would have blamed him. For seven years, he labored in India as a missionary. In those seven years, his son died of dysentery, his wife suffered a nervous breakdown, his friends misunderstood his vision and would not support it, and no one got saved. But Carey had an expectation. He famously said, "Expect great things from God; attempt great things for God."

At the end of his life, Carey could look back and see many people saved, the Bible translated and printed into forty Indian dialects, a Bible college built, and more missionaries coming to India and to other countries around the world. Carey once said, "We have only to keep the end in view, and have our hearts thoroughly engaged in the pursuit of it."[4] He had set his expectation on God and his eyes on the goal, and India is changed today as a result.

God Comes to Enlarge Your Expectation

Are you a person whose expectations are too little? You might have small expectations because of your circumstances, your past, your family tree, or your own failures or sense of limitations, but do not allow these things to limit your expectation. Remember that you are the general contractor of your life. You may get shipped some bad bricks and weak steel, but it is your choice whether you will build with the faulty materials or go to God for good building materials. Do you build with what others say about your future or with what God says about your future? Do you build with God's promises or with your past failures?

When Albert Einstein was fifteen years old, his teacher told his parents, "It doesn't matter what he does, he will never amount to anything." Einstein had a choice. He could build his life with those words, or he could find different words with which to build. The choice he made is clear.

The ultimate quality of your life expectation is determined by your willingness to take responsibility for who you are becoming. Get rid of the victim mentality. It will cripple your soul. Don't repeat the victim's lament, "I can't help myself. It's not my fault. It's because of...." Don't blame your life's limits on other people. Don't make excuses. Rise up and expect great things from God, from yourself, and from life.

Personal Testimony

Royce and Elizabeth,
Missionaries to Uganda in Their Forties

They were both successful businesspeople with comfortable lifestyles. Two years ago, with two children in elementary school, they left it all to follow God's call.

Having been fed years of faith-filled, "can-do" teaching, we were eventually challenged to climb out of life's comfortable boat and jump into unknown waters. Our family enjoyed a blessed life—involved in church and our children's schooling, enjoying rich friendships, and working hard in business. Yet God began to rearrange our values and priorities. We realized that faith is meaningless to God unless it leads to action! He was encouraging us to invest our lives, by faith, toward things we couldn't yet see.

So, trusting God, we left the comfortable and familiar and embraced an uncertain future. With one-way tickets in hand, our family boarded a plane to an unknown country to serve a people we had yet to meet. God's plans are always greater than we imagine, but many are unwilling to pay the price to see them realized, or they quit before faith becomes sight.

Our faith journey hasn't been rewarded with an easy walk or instant results. In fact, most of the time, when you begin to act on a new level of faith, you can expect to meet resistance and discouragement. We have faced harsh living conditions, numerous rounds with malaria, broken bones, delayed dreams, and ongoing cultural stress and rejection. Stepping out in faith has cost us everything that was dear to our way of life. There's nothing pleasant about chasing bats out of your room at night, listening to water dripping from a leaking grass roof, sleeping under nets, or facing human suffering on a daily basis.

Where do you get the courage to serve one more day? Our *perspective* changed—we had to be willing to take our eyes off this temporary life, believe God rewards faith, and be willing to invest in eternity. Also, we are learning that great *patience* is needed to walk by faith. Payday isn't today! We don't need to see results now, and, to be honest, we might have to wait until eternity to see the fullness of service. In doing so, we endure the hard stuff, because in spite of what we see, *He always rewards faith!*

God Comes to Restore Your Perspective When You Are Discouraged

Expectation is especially needed among those who are discouraged and have lost perspective. God wants to help you gain new

> *When you gain an eternal perspective, the temporal loses its hold on you.*

perspective on this temporal world in which we live. When you gain an eternal perspective, the temporal loses its hold on you. In reality, the things that seem so important now are only small blips on the screen of life.

Did you know that birds can see out of only one eye at a time? That's why birds are always cocking their heads to look at things. Scientists have discovered that a bird gets a different perspective depending on which eye it is using. With one eye it detects movement and with the other it detects color, so its perspective varies greatly depending on which eye it uses. Our perspectives also depend on what eyes we look through—our natural eyes or our spiritual eyes. When we see life through God-glasses, we see things clearly and can put everything in perspective.

One of the greatest deterrents to expectation is discouragement. The discouraged person has a distorted view of circumstances and life in general. A discouraged person loses heart and expectation for anything good in life. Discouragement comes for a variety of reasons. For example, you can become discouraged when you see good things happening to bad people. They prosper financially, have abundant possessions, and seem to have wonderful lives.

Then, you see bad things happen to good people who serve and love God but do not prosper in life, do not have enough of anything, and seem to be treated poorly by life. When people who trust God, serve God, and love God experience extreme hardships, troubles, and losses, it does not make sense. Why should you expect good things from God if even the "good" people cannot expect good things?

When you see the innocent suffering and the evil going unpunished, you can lose perspective. You must come to grips with this and put your eyes back on God and His Word.

> *But as for me, my feet had almost stumbled; my steps had nearly slipped. For I was envious of the boastful, when I saw the prosperity of the wicked.*   (Psalm 73:2–3)

When I thought how to understand this, it was too painful for me; until I went into the sanctuary of God; then I understood their end. (Psalm 73:16–17)

If you take your eyes off the faithfulness of God, your dreams will die—and a life without dreams is a life without hope. As poet Langston Hughes said,

> Hold fast to dreams,
> For if dreams die,
> Life is a broken-winged bird
> That cannot fly.
>
> Hold fast to dreams,
> For when dreams go,
> Life is a barren field,
> Frozen with snow.[5]

When expectation is lost, life is reduced to boredom and an attitude of "whatever happens, happens."

God's Plans Are Greater Than You May Know

Allen Gardiner had a dream of taking the gospel to the Yagan tribe of Patagonia (the southern region of South America). He founded the Patagonian Missionary Society and traveled to the southern tip of South America to reach the Yagan tribe. Through a series of misfortunes, he ended up dying alone in Tierra del Fuego. Yet, his dream was preserved in the journal found beside his dead body.

As Gardiner lay dying, he wrote out his vision to expand the Patagonian Missionary Society to become the South American Missionary Society and enlarge the dream from merely reaching Patagonia to reaching the entire continent. The fruit of his life and dream is seen in a mission society that is still active today and a Yagan tribe that has been transformed by the gospel. Painted on a rock on the beach where he died are words from Psalm 62:5: *"My soul, wait thou only upon God; for my expectation is from him"* (KJV).

God Has His Hand on Your Life

In Mark 1:29–31, we read of the incident where Peter's mother-in-law lay sick with fever and Jesus came to the house to help her. It says, *"He came and took her by the hand and lifted her up, and immediately the fever left her. And she served them"* (verse 31). Jesus desires to visit your life, to take you by the hand, and to lift you out of all that is holding you back. Reach out and give Him your hand.

> *When God visits someone, it is to care for that person and to bring him or her into something good.*

When God visits someone, it is to care for that person and to bring him or her into something good. (See, for example, Genesis 21:1; Ruth 1:6; 1 Samuel 2:21; Luke 19:44.) God desires to put His hand on you and bring His power and His presence into your life. The mighty hand of God is coming to you. Open up your life and let God visit you.

God's hand on you is His hand of promotion to lift you to another level of influence and fruitfulness. God's hand on you is His hand of provision, providing you with everything you need—spiritually, mentally, emotionally, financially, and physically. God's hand on you is His hand of protection, a divine hedge built around your life, a wall of fire to keep out all that would seek to harm or destroy. God's hand on you is His hand of power, providing strength for you to fulfill the dreams that He has given you.

Psalm 139:5 declares, *"You have hedged me behind and before, and laid Your hand upon me."* (See also Deuteronomy 5:15; Ezra 8:31; 1 Peter 5:6.)

A Right Perspective Sees God's Hand at Work

God desires to put His hand on you, and He desires to speak personally to you. We need to open our ears to hear.

The Lord GOD has given Me the tongue of the learned, that
I should know how to speak a word in season to him who is
weary. He awakens Me morning by morning, He awakens My
ear to hear as the learned. The Lord GOD has opened My ear;
and I was not rebellious, nor did I turn away. (Isaiah 50:4–5)

God will speak to you uniquely, personally, progressively, consistently, faithfully, unmistakably, and powerfully. God will speak
to you by His written Word. Read it. He will speak to you by His
quickened Word. Pray it. And He will speak to you by His Holy
Spirit. Listen carefully.

Regaining Perspective in the Presence of God

One of the truths that Allen Gardiner understood was the power
of the presence of God to maintain perspective in difficult times. In
one of his final journal entries, he wrote, "We feel and know that
God is here. Asleep or awake, I am, beyond the power of expression, happy."[6]

You can recover a right perspective by basking in the presence of
God. Go into your hiding place—the place of protection and cover-
ing of God that the psalmist refers to in the Bible.

You shall hide them in the secret place of Your presence from the
plots of man; You shall keep them secretly in a pavilion from the
strife of tongues. (Psalm 31:20)

Keep me as the apple of Your eye; hide me under the shadow of
Your wings. (Psalm 17:8)

The presence of God is your place
of refuge and your place to be revived in
heart and spirit. Your place of prayer and
praise is the hiding place where you find
the presence of God. It is the time and
place where you focus on God and have a
fresh encounter with Him. The personal
presence of God is not merely a force or

> *The presence of*
> *God is your place*
> *of refuge and your*
> *place to be revived*
> *in heart and spirit.*

influence; it is a personal, real, life-changing power. Moses' prayer is also the prayer of a person of expectation:

> *He said, "My Presence will go with you, and I will give you rest." Then he said to Him, "If Your Presence does not go with us, do not bring us up from here. For how then will it be known that Your people and I have found grace in Your sight, except You go with us? So we shall be separate, Your people and I, from all the people who are upon the face of the earth."*
> (Exodus 33:14–16)

The presence of God becomes the reviving power of vision and expectation. It becomes the air you breathe, and it supercharges your spiritual batteries. The psalmist affirms, *"You will show me the path of life; in Your presence is fullness of joy; at Your right hand are pleasures forevermore"* (Psalm 16:11). God's will is that you should press into His presence and live your whole life there. This is more than a doctrine to be held; it is a life to be enjoyed.

Making a Place for the Presence of God

Making a place for God's empowering presence must become your first passion if you are to stay full of hope and expectation. Expectation will not grow in the shallowness of your inner experience. You must go deeper. God seeks to commune with you, to confirm His Word to your spirit, to inspire you to do great and mighty things, and to impart courage, faith, and new vision to you.

Make Christ Your Personal Savior

To partake of God's rich and marvelous presence in your life, you must find Christ as your personal Savior and Lord. Ask yourself some simple questions. *Have I been born again by the Spirit of God? Have I confessed that I am a sinner, repented, asked forgiveness for all my sins, accepted Christ's work for me on the cross, and received God's free gift of eternal life?* (See Romans 8:16; Revelation 3:20.) *Has Christ taken up residence in my life with the Holy Spirit, speaking to me and revealing things to me? Is God's power and presence driving my life?*

Make a Secret Place to Be Alone with God

We are a generation of Christians who have been raised in a world of push buttons, automatic machines, and fast technology. We have drive-through restaurants for fast food, drive-through ATMs for fast money, and drive-through pharmacies for fast pre-scriptions. We want everything to be immediate. Unfortunately, we try to carry this fast mentality over into our relationship with God by employing quick devotions, quick Bible readings, and quick prayers.

God wants us to shut ourselves away and spend time with Him, to separate ourselves from the distractions and rush of life. He wants to develop a one-on-one relationship with you that is just you and Him, not you and everyone else. Do not depend on others to hear God's voice for you. Set aside time to sit and listen to hear what He has to say directly to you. Close the door and shut out all distracting voices, tuning your heart to hear His voice.

> *Do not depend on others to hear God's voice for you.*

The hiding place, or secret place to be alone with God, is not a special room that you build in your house. It is the place that you create when you shut out the world and focus on God. You can make a secret place anywhere. With nineteen children, Susanna Wesley, the mother of evangelists John and Charles Wesley, knew what busy-ness was. Yet she made her secret place with God a priority in her life. She would sit in her kitchen and put her apron over her face. That was a sign to the children that she was alone with God and was not to be bothered. Amid the hubbub of the household, she focused her atten-tion on talking with God.

Let's examine some words of wisdom about prayer in the secret place.

Prayer is so simple. It is like quietly opening a door and slip-ping into the very presence of God. There, in the stillness, to listen to His voice, perhaps in petition or only to listen. It matters not. Just to be there in His presence is prayer.[7]

St. Bernard said,

Wherever therefore thou shalt be, pray secretly within thyself. If thou shalt be far from a house of prayer, give not thyself trouble to seek one. For thou thyself art a sanctuary designed for prayer.[8]

Andrew Murray said that your secret place is where you...

Shut the world out, withdraw from all worldly thoughts and occupations, and shut yourself in alone with God, to pray to Him in secret. Let this be your chief object in prayer: *to realize the presence of your heavenly Father.* Let your watchword be: Alone with God.[9]

Make a Life of Prayer

Do not limit your time with God to a measured allotment of your day. God is not someone to be written into your daybook and then restricted to that specific appointment time. God desires that you live in communion with Him all the time—every minute, every hour, every day, every week, every month, every year, for your entire life. Brother Lawrence was a seventeenth-century monk who wrote a simple but profound book called *The Practice of the Presence of God.* He said,

I make it my priority to persevere in His holy presence, wherein I maintain a simple attention and a fond regard for God, which I may call an actual presence of God. Or, to put it another way, it is a habitual, silent, and private conversation of the soul with God.[10]

> *To practice the presence of God is to live in the conscious awareness of your Father.*

To practice the presence of God is to live in the conscious awareness of your Father, engaging in quiet, joyful, and continuous conversation with Him. It means that you live an inner life of unceasing prayer (see 1 Thessalonians 5:17) and that you strive for all you think, say, and do to be a reflection of what is pleasing to God (see 1 Thessalonians 2:4). God is not a future goal or a past memory, but a right-this-second presence in your life.

Expectation is fueled by spending time in God's presence. Expectation is set aflame by the empowering Spirit of the living God. The place for God's presence is not just the position of standing in God's presence, but it is the driving force in the daily lives of God's servants. A. W. Tozer said,

> It is not mere words that nourish the soul, but God Himself, and unless and until the hearers find God in personal experience, they are not the better for having heard the truth.[12]

Make an Altar before God

Whenever Abraham moved to a new place, the first thing he would do was build an altar. In Genesis 12, he moved to Schechem and *"built an altar to the Lᴏʀᴅ"* (verse 7). Then, in verse 8, we learn that he moved to Bethel and built an altar again. Later, in chapter 13, he moved to Hebron, and in verse 18, we are told that he built another altar to the Lord. The altar was the place where he *"called on the name of the Lᴏʀᴅ"* (Genesis 12:8). Abraham recognized the importance of making a place for meeting with God a priority in his life.

If you built a stone altar in your backyard and went out there every morning to pray, you would probably be the talk of your neighborhood! As Christians today, we don't need to construct physical altars. Rather, the principle is about making a place in your life that is set apart to God—a place where you meet with Him on a daily basis. Andrew Murray said,

> We need a period daily for secret fellowship. Time to turn from daily occupation and search our hearts in His presence. Time to study His Word with reverence and godly fear. Time to seek His face and ask Him to make Himself known to us. Time to wait until we know that He sees and hears us so that we can make our wants known to Him in words that come from the depth of our hearts. Time to let God deal

with our special needs, to let His light shine in our hearts, to let ourselves be filled with His Spirit![12]

God wants to meet with you. He desires for you to live in the power of His presence. His presence in your life is a reality. It is personal, and it is for you—right now and right where you are. Build that place through prayer. It may not be easy. It does take discipline. According to Henri Nouwen,

> Spiritual life without discipline is impossible. Discipline is the other side of discipleship. The practice of spiritual discipline makes us more sensitive to the small, gentle voice of God.[13]

Remember, the focus of making a secret place is to meet with God and build your relationship with Him. Take time to read your Bible every day, whether it is two verses or two chapters. Take time to talk with God and to listen to Him. After all, conversation is a two-way street! That principle is just as true with God as it is with our families or friends.

Meditate on the things that you read and the things that God speaks to you in prayer and through His Word. Take those verses with you throughout the day and think about them. Make Bible reading and prayer parts of your everyday life. The apostle Paul said it like this:

> *Take your everyday, ordinary life—your sleeping, eating, going-to-work, and walking-around life—and place it before God as an offering....Fix your attention on God. You'll be changed from the inside out.* (Romans 12:1–2 MSG)

Chapter 3

Yes to the God-Thought

God has thoughts for your life. They are not small thoughts for a limited future but great thoughts for a great future. Your expectation will be raised to a new level when you begin to grasp God's thoughts about you and for you. In Isaiah 55:8–9, God said,

> *For My thoughts are not your thoughts, nor are your ways My ways....For as the heavens are higher than the earth, so are My ways higher than your ways, and My thoughts than your thoughts.*

Your expectation will be raised to a new level when you begin to grasp God's thoughts about you and for you.

God thinks differently about your life than you do. He thinks differently about His promises and what He would like to put into your hands and do through your life. His way of thinking is as high above your thinking as the heavens are above the earth.

Just think sixty miles straight up. That's how far the heavens are from the earth—that's the beginning of space. To break through that barrier and reach space requires traveling at seven miles per second, or 25,000 miles per hour. To accomplish this, space shuttles use two solid rocket boosters that contain more than one million pounds of fuel each. Just think: as high as the heavens are from the earth, that is how much higher God's thoughts are toward you than your thoughts toward yourself!

God is thinking about you; understanding His thoughts toward you will help you achieve what is in His heart and mind. God desires to speak clearly because He has specific objectives that He has purposed for your life, and He does not want you to miss any of His thoughts. It is to our benefit to know God's thoughts toward us and to hear His voice when He speaks.

Luke 2:19 says, *"Mary kept all these things and pondered them in her heart."* To ponder something is to weigh it in the mind, to think deeply and carefully about it, to consider it soberly, to meditate on it, or to examine it attentively. When we focus on God's thoughts toward us, it is more than just daydreaming—it is a deliberate search for the thoughts of God. (See Proverbs 4:26; Psalm 77:12.) In Isaiah 55:8–9, God said,

> *"I don't think the way you think. The way you work isn't the way I work." God's Decree. "For as the sky soars high above earth, so the way I work surpasses the way you work, and the way I think is beyond the way you think."* (MSG)

God's thoughts are higher thoughts, above-average thoughts, important thoughts. And, as Jeremiah says, they are good thoughts.

> *For I know the thoughts that I think toward you, says the LORD, thoughts of peace and not of evil, to give you a future and a hope.*
> (Jeremiah 29:11)

Think Higher Thoughts

In Philippians 3:14, Paul said, *"I press toward the goal for the prize of the upward call of God in Christ Jesus."* It is a high call, a high thought. Do not set your target low and aim at an inferior calling. Allow God to quicken His Word to you and push your thoughts higher. Let the fuel of His presence propel you toward His thoughts for your life. God wants to pour His Spirit into your heart and mind to give you high expectations. You are more than a conqueror. You can break bad habits. You can do great things. You can be a mighty man or woman of valor through God.

The Word of the Lord comes in and stirs you to higher expectation—to believe what God says and to raise your vision to His vision. Rise up and take what is yours. Do not sit back and allow life to pass by. Get up and take hold of the promises of God. Get up and pursue the vision that God has placed in your heart.

You may have forgotten the dream you used to have, but God hasn't. You may not believe in the dream anymore, but He does. He believes in the dream, and He believes in you. He has been working on you and your dream the whole time. It may have been a long time. Many years may have passed since you first began to dream the dream. You may have lost many precious things. You may have lost hope. The dream may have faded from delay after delay. But mark this down: it's not over yet!

> *You may have forgotten the dream you used to have, but God hasn't.*

Personal Testimony

Faith,
Teacher, Widow, Missionary to Indonesia in Her Sixties

As young college students, Jack and Faith felt called by God to go to Indonesia as missionaries, but their first steps led them to pastor a church and then work at a Christian rehabilitation center with alcoholics and drug addicts. Over the next twenty-five years, they often prayed together, "Is now the time for the dream to be fulfilled?" Each time, God said, "Not yet. Your work here is not done." For twenty-five years, they prayed about the dream, and for twenty-five years, they waited. Then, Jack died of cancer. What would happen to the dream now?

For the next several years, Faith focused on raising her children and finishing school to get her degree in education. The dream was forgotten in the struggles of being a single mom and facing life without her husband. But God began to stir the dream again. Faith argued with Him. How could she go into the mission field by herself? She was too afraid to try this alone. She needed Jack. But the dream that had been planted forty years earlier began to burn again in her spirit, and forty years after she and Jack had shared their dream to go to Indonesia, Faith stepped foot onto Indonesian soil for the first time in her life. As a widow of sixty, she fulfilled the dream of the twenty-year-old woman.

What are the obstacles that stand in your way? What are the detours that time has led you down? How many years have passed since the birth of your dream? Right now, say to yourself, *It's not over yet!* Your age, status in life, gender, and abilities do not matter. What is God saying? What are His thoughts? It's not over until the will of God has been done.

God's Thoughts Change Your Life

"For I know the thoughts that I think toward you, says the LORD*..."* (Jeremiah 29:11). What are God's thoughts toward us? Wouldn't it be awesome to be able to put on headphones and listen to a recording of God's thoughts toward you right now? Just imagine if you could plug in and listen to His thoughts about your future—His thoughts about your dream and your vision! *Wow, that's an awesome thought! That's amazing!*

Have you ever sat next to someone who was listening to music with earphones on the bus or on a plane? You usually can't hear anything, but you know that person is listening to music by the way his head is bobbing, his mouth is moving to words you can't hear, and his whole body is in synch with an unheard beat. He might look ridiculous. You sit there and laugh at him because his actions are out of synch with the world around him. But if you could hear what he is hearing, you would probably be doing the same thing he is doing.

That's the way it is with the thoughts of God. If you start hearing the thoughts of God—hearing what the Lord wants to do in you and through you—then you will start moving differently. You will begin to respond differently, walk differently, and talk differently. You will be living in a different realm—the realm of God-thoughts.

God Desires to Communicate with You

God is speaking to you continually, using every possible way for you to hear and understand His voice. God has spoken through angels, prophets, dreams, visions, creation, and a still, small voice. He has spoken through a burning bush, signs and miracles, fleeces, writing on the wall, impressions, quickened Scriptures, people, circumstances, and the Holy Spirit.

> *God is speaking to you continually, using every possible way for you to hear and understand His voice.*

God wants to tell you His thoughts about you. They are His unique, specific thoughts designed just for you. He wants to talk directly to you about your immediate needs, your questions about life, and the decisions you need to make.

God's thoughts toward you are innumerable. You cannot measure them. The psalmist marveled,

> *How precious are your thoughts about me, O God. They cannot be numbered! I can't even count them; they outnumber the grains of sand! And when I wake up, you are still with me!*
> (Psalm 139:17–18 NLT)

In the *New King James Version*, verse 18 reads, *"If I should count them, they would be more in number than the sand."* Some mathematicians at the University of Hawaii tried to figure out how many grains of sand are on the world's beaches. They estimated that there are approximately 7,500,000,000,000,000,000 (seven quintillion, five quadrillion) grains of sand. And that doesn't even come close to how much God is thinking about you!

God's thoughts toward you are inestimable. *"How precious also are Your thoughts to me, O God!"* (verse 17). They are invaluable, beyond any price, and of supreme worth. They are awesome thoughts to encourage you, inspire you to greatness, and cause you to hit the mark He has set for you.

How vast is the sum of God's thoughts! He isn't stingy with His thoughts. He doesn't give you a thought once every five, ten, or fifteen years. His thoughts are vast and innumerable. He has so many thoughts that you cannot even imagine how many are coming your way.

God's thoughts toward you are timely. He desires to give you the precise word you need for the precise time you need it. He wants to give you a *now* word for a *now* time so that you might know and understand the plans and designs of an ever-present and all-powerful God. They are specific words for a specific time and for a specific purpose.

How long has it been since you had a penetrating, lifting-up-and-getting-on-with-it thought from God? How long has it been since a thought impacted you so deeply that it changed the way you lived? How long since you heard a thought that changed the way you viewed life or changed the way you considered yourself? How long since you have been impacted by a God-thought?

When you get a God-thought, you scramble for a pen and immediately begin to write it down. When was the last time you got out of bed at night, turned on the light, and began writing down a thought from God? When was the last time you pulled over on the side of the road to write down what God was speaking into your heart on the way to work? When was the last time you heard a thought from God?

You must listen carefully and diligently to God's thoughts toward you. Pay attention to what He is saying and wait patiently and passionately for His thoughts and words. Listen for God's thoughts because His ways are vastly superior to your ways and your thoughts. Your greatest thoughts will always be inferior to God's thoughts for you.

God's Thoughts in Motion toward You

Let's look at different translations of this verse, Psalm 139:17: *"How precious also are Your thoughts to me, O God! How great is the sum of them!"* In *The Message*, this verse reads, *"Your thoughts—how rare, how beautiful! God, I'll never comprehend them!*" The *Amplified Bible* expounds, "*How precious and weighty also are Your thoughts to me, O God! How vast is the sum of them!*" In the *New Living Translation*, it reads, "*How precious are your thoughts about me, O God. They cannot be numbered!*"

The Hebrew word for *thought* encompasses the idea of intentions, purposes, designs, thoughts, and dreams. It refers to the thoughts and purposes that fill a person's mind. God has many great thoughts about you and for you. They are thoughts that will bring high expectations to your life.

> *Many, O LORD my God, are Your wonderful works which You have done; and Your thoughts toward us cannot be recounted to You in order; if I would declare and speak of them, they are more than can be numbered.* (Psalm 40:5)

When you consider the thoughts of God, put the following four phrases to work, because the thoughts of God involve all of them:

- God's intentions for your life.
- God's purposes for your life.
- God's designs for your life.
- God's dreams for your life.

Receive the Thoughts of God

When you begin to hear the intentions of God for your life, see His purposes and designs, hear His thoughts, and see His dreams, you begin to change. You begin to expect different things in life. You begin to live differently. You change the way you think, the way you act, and the way you perceive.

When you begin to hear the intentions of God for your life, you begin to change.

God's thoughts are "*toward*" you. They are thoughts that are in motion, coming your way. God is throwing, hurling, casting His thoughts in your direction. They are not just one or two thoughts, but too many to count, innumerable, and more than can be numbered. They are thoughts of grace, love, forgiveness, purpose, calling, and provision. They are all being hurled toward you. Won't you stop and catch them? Receive them? Capture them?

Have you ever stood outside in a snowstorm and looked up at the big flakes falling toward you? Picture those flakes tumbling down as the thoughts of God coming to you. That is how many thoughts are coming your way. Thousands! More than thousands! More than seven quintillion, five quadrillion thoughts!

Do you remember playing catch when you were a child? I played baseball when I was in school, so it's the sport I always wanted my kids to play. Whether boys or girls, my children had to have baseballs when they were little. At first, I would roll the baseball to them. As soon as they got big enough to stand up, I would bounce it to them. When they got bigger, I would throw it to them so they could catch it. It wasn't easy for them to learn. They would stand with their hands wide apart, waiting for it.

"Put your hands together. Like this. Okay, now just catch it. I'll throw it right into your hands. You just catch it."

But they would open their hands and let it fall between them, or they would fall down and the ball would bounce off their heads. Still, I kept throwing it and they kept trying until they caught the ball every time I threw it.

The thoughts of God are coming your way today. He has some thoughts that He is pitching toward you. "Here they come, son. Here they come, daughter. Here's a thought. Get your hands ready. Put that faith mitt on. Get ready to catch it. I'm throwing some things your way, and I want you to catch them. Are you ready?"

Waiting for God's Thoughts

Here's a thought from God. It's coming. Reach out and catch it.

But to catch it, you must be ready for it. So how can we be ready? The Bible says that we must wait on the Lord, listen to His voice, and be open to hear what He has to say. (See Psalm 27:14.) But so often, we stand with our arms folded and frowns on our faces, saying, "Give it your best shot, God. Nice pitch, but I just don't believe it. I'm not even going to try to catch it because the last time I did, nothing happened. I've caught those thoughts before, and they didn't change anything, so why try now? From now on, I'm just going to stand here with my arms folded. If You want me to catch a thought, You'll have to beat me on the head with it. Then, maybe I'll believe it."

Right now, ask God to forgive you for the attitude of unbelief and the reluctance to receive His thoughts. Then, put up your faith mitt and begin to wait on Him. Begin to read the Scriptures and listen to the Holy Spirit. His thoughts are toward you. He desires to speak His thoughts to you because His thoughts are unique, inspired, and awesome. They are powerful, far superior to our thoughts for life. They can fill your whole being. They push out the darkness, push out the negativity, and push out the smallness of the soul and the flesh. They push out the non-God-thoughts from your life so that you have a new fire, a new passion, and a new understanding of His will for you.

God's thoughts are unique, inspired, and awesome. They are far superior to our thoughts for life.

Personal Testimony

Cheryl,
Thirty Years Old

God began speaking to me one day about working on my Spanish. I had studied Spanish for four years in high school, so I enrolled in a college class. God kept speaking and stirring my spirit. That was not enough. So, I enrolled in a two-week immersion course in Ecuador.

As the plane landed in Ecuador, my thoughts were quite simple: *What in the world possessed you to do something like this? There are lots of missionaries you know in places where you could have gone for a few weeks to practice Spanish. You could have started attending a Spanish service at home. Now, you are living with strangers who you know nothing about! What you have gotten yourself into?* Thankfully, God had different thoughts in mind.

On my second day there, I realized why God had directed me to this place and at this time. My speaking lesson consisted of a two-hour conversation each day with a young teacher named Priscilla. On the second day of the class, she interrupted the language lesson with a question: "If God forgives me, is it forever?" For the next week, we talked about the gospel every day, and at the end of the week, she began a personal relationship with Christ. During the second week, we talked about developing that relationship with God.

So, why did God send me to that place at that time? My life was changed as I gained the confidence of knowing that language was not a barrier to sharing the gospel, and Priscilla's life was changed for eternity.

God's Thoughts toward You Are Unique

God has unique, specific thoughts that are designed just for you—for a specific time and a specific purpose. You aren't receiving the afterthoughts that are left over after God thinks about somebody else. He doesn't have leftover thoughts from thinking about Billy Graham that He tosses toward you. He has specific thoughts for your life. He has specific thoughts for this exact time and season in your life.

God desires to reveal His innumerable, awesome thoughts toward you with the goal of encouraging you and inspiring you to greatness. He wants you to hit the mark He has set for you in life. When God sends thoughts toward you, they change your life. They alter the way you live. They change your direction and make you more fruitful, and you begin to live like the overcomer He says you are. (See Romans 8:37.)

God desires to communicate His thoughts directly to you concerning your immediate needs, your future questions about life, and the decisions you need to make. You do not have to twist His arm to get Him to toss His thoughts your way. He desires to speak to you. He desires to touch your life. He cares about you as an individual and wants to speak directly to you.

He also wants you to listen carefully and diligently to what He has to say. He wants you to wait patiently and passionately for His thoughts and words. He wants you to stand ready to hear. Live with a pencil in hand, always ready to write down what He is saying. Maybe you cannot do this literally, but you can do it in your spirit. You can maintain an attitude of alertness, an ear that is always open and listening, and a heart that is ready to receive and write into your life what God speaks.

Discerning the Thoughts Aimed toward You

There are many thoughts aimed toward you in life. Some are good, and others are not good. You must learn to discern between the thoughts from God and the thoughts from other sources.

> *You must learn to discern between the thoughts from God and the thoughts from other sources.*

Discerning Wrong Thoughts from Your Carnal Mind

There are thoughts that come from your own limited, carnal mind. They must be rejected and put out of your life because *"the carnal mind is enmity against God; for it is not subject to the law of God, nor indeed can be"* (Romans 8:7). The carnal mind is set on fulfilling the desires of the flesh—your lower nature, the sin-driven part of you that seeks to control you. This lower sinful nature cares only for sinful interests and has no regard for God. Thoughts from the carnal mind will drive you to fulfill carnal ambitions and ruin your life.

The sinful nature and the indwelling Spirit of God are in conflict. According to Galatians 5:17,

> *For the flesh lusts against the Spirit, and the Spirit against the flesh; and these are contrary to one another, so that you do not do the things that you wish.*

The carnal mind is hostile to God (see Romans 5:10) and does not submit to God's laws or God's way. Reject the thoughts that originate in the carnal mind.

Discerning Wrong Thoughts from Negative Thinking

There are thoughts in motion toward you from your past that must be rejected. The ruts of negative thinking are strongholds that will cause you to miss the thoughts of God coming to you. People with negative thinking are masters of illusion. Their pessimistic outlooks can turn triumphs into setbacks and setbacks into personal failures. Negative thinking can cause depression and plague you with doubts about yourself and your future. This kind of thinking distorts your view of the world until everything seems dreary and hopeless.

The thoughts you allow into your life shape your moods into hopelessness or into high hope and expectation. God-thoughts translate into positive thoughts that transform your life with energy, hope, and faith. But when you allow the negative thoughts to find a place in your mind, you set up a stronghold of negative thinking.

> *For the weapons of our warfare are not carnal but mighty in God for pulling down strongholds, casting down arguments and every high thing that exalts itself against the knowledge of God, bringing every thought into captivity to the obedience of Christ, and being ready to punish all disobedience when your obedience is fulfilled.* (2 Corinthians 10:4–6)

Negative thinking cripples your spirit and diminishes your expectation level. This insidious disease, which I call *negativitis* (negative thinking), must be rooted out of your life and destroyed. You are called to greatness by God's grace, and God's thoughts toward you are wonderful.

There are many who have been crippled, damaged, and broken and who plod along aimlessly with dark clouds brooding over them. They are like Charlie Brown's friend Pigpen in the *Peanuts* comic strip by Charles M. Schulz. Everywhere Pigpen went, a cloud of dust followed and surrounded him, tainting everything he touched. That is not you! Reject that way of living!

Quit complaining about what you do not have and start seeing what you do have. Complaining just digs the rut deeper and deeper, making it increasingly difficult to climb out of the ditch you've created. To climb out, you must grab hold of the God-thoughts that are coming toward you. Do not shift the blame and make someone else responsible for the way you are. Complaining and blame shifting lead to negative thinking and are self-defeating.

Today is the day for you to take hold of the God-thoughts for your life. Admit into your mind the thoughts, words, and images that are conducive to growth, change, miracles, hope, vision, dreams, and expectations. Expect good and favorable results from your prayers and expect to see the hand of God over your life. Anticipate breakthroughs in life. Anticipate joy. Anticipate a successful outcome of your situation. Reject the negative thoughts and grab hold of the God-thoughts.

This may take time and discipline, but you *will* overcome the negative thoughts and negative expectations. Persevere, and you can transform the way your mind thinks. When a negative thought enters your mind, be aware of it and replace it with a God-thought. Do not give up on this. You will overcome!

When a negative thought enters your mind, be aware of it and replace it with a God-thought.

Discerning Wrong Thoughts from the Enemy of Your Soul

There are thoughts in motion toward you from the enemy of your soul, the devil. Ephesians 6 tells us,

> *For we do not wrestle against flesh and blood, but against principalities, against powers, against the rulers of the darkness of this age, against spiritual hosts of wickedness in the heavenly places....Above all, taking the shield of faith with which you will be able to quench all the fiery darts of the wicked one. And take*

the helmet of salvation, and the sword of the Spirit, which is the
word of God. (Ephesians 6:12, 16–17)

The thoughts being hurled at you from the devil are usually twisted lies that seek to ensnare you and stop you from becoming all that God has called you to be. The devil uses lying thoughts and false statements that are deliberately presented as true. They are sent to deceive you or give you the wrong impression. The devil's lies are hurled at you to lead you astray and destroy the good work of God in your life.

Have you heard these common lies hurled toward you?

- You are not totally forgiven.
- You are never going to succeed at anything.
- You will never change, so why keep trying?
- Your past failures have limited your future.
- Your destiny is not as bright as that of others.
- You married the wrong person.
- Your prayers are useless.
- You will never love again.
- You can get away with it, so go ahead and do whatever you want to do.

When these thoughts come to you, you need to remember what God's Word says about the devil. He is a liar and the father of lies.

You are of your father the devil, and the desires of your father
you want to do. He was a murderer from the beginning, and
does not stand in the truth, because there is no truth in him.
When he speaks a lie, he speaks from his own resources, for he
is a liar and the father of it. (John 8:44)

The devil brought spiritual and physical death to humanity with a lie. (See Genesis 3:4, 13; 1 John 3:8, 10–15.) He is the distorter of truth and will always seek to lead you away from the truth and away from God. Reject his lies. Resist his invasion. You were meant to live out God-thoughts toward you.

Discerning Wrong Thoughts from Other People

Discern the thoughts coming toward you from people with limited faith and limited God-knowledge. There are thoughts toward you from people who know you—such as parents, friends, or teachers—but who don't know what God has put in your heart. They may not have faith in God's dream for you. They don't know what God has spoken into your heart. Be careful not to let them shape your soul or steal your seeds of expectation. People can be cruel with their words, or they can simply be careless with them. Guard your mind and resist the wrong thoughts coming from those around you.

Such people are like David's brother. David was bringing lunch to his brothers, who were stationed on the front lines of the battle. He saw Goliath screaming and yelling, blaspheming God. David asked, "What's with that uncircumcised Philistine over there?" (See 1 Samuel 17:26.) The soldiers just shrugged. They were used to hearing Goliath's taunts; who wants to aggravate an angry bully twice his size?

But David was a giant killer in the making. He was a man of God in the making. His heart was different from theirs. He had a heart that ran to the challenge. His brothers couldn't identify with that, so they told him, "Go back and take care of your sheep, David. You're a proud little sheep boy. You just came to see the battle. You don't understand what's going on here. Go back to the things you know—your sheep." (See 1 Samuel 17:28, 33.)

They couldn't understand a giant-killing heart. They couldn't understand the heart of a boy who was becoming a king. Sometimes, people will say things to you that are wrong, limited, or critical. They want to shrink you to fit their world. Don't answer them back. Don't get angry at them. Just smile and say, "…but God." Remember that phrase: *but God*. "*But God* is in this, so it can work. *But God* said, so I can."

> *Sometimes, people will say things to you that are limited or critical. Don't get angry at them. Just smile and say, "…but God."*

Discerning the Thoughts of God toward You

Discern the God-thoughts in motion toward you right now. He is always thinking about you, and His thoughts are good. Psalm 16:6 says, *"The lines have fallen to me in pleasant places; yes, I have a good inheritance."* Psalm 21:3 says, *"You meet him with the blessings of goodness; You set a crown of pure gold upon his head."*

God's goodness will follow you for your entire life. Psalm 23:6 says, *"Surely goodness and mercy shall follow me all the days of my life; and I will dwell in the house of the LORD forever."*

When God forgives you, He does not remember the sins of your youth. Psalm 25:7 says, *"Do not remember the sins of my youth, nor my transgressions; according to Your mercy remember me, for Your goodness' sake, O LORD."*

When life seems overwhelming and you feel like giving up, put those fears behind you and receive the good things of God. Psalm 27:13 says, *"I would have lost heart, unless I had believed that I would see the goodness of the LORD in the land of the living."* Psalm 33:5 says, *"He loves righteousness and justice; the earth is full of the goodness of the LORD."*

Here are some of God's thoughts toward you from His quickened Word:

- I have your life written out in My Book. I have had plans for you, even before you were born. I have had you in My heart always. (See Psalm 139:16.)
- I have forgiven you of everything in your past and removed your sins from you as far as the east is from the west. (See Psalm 103:12.)
- I have destined for you to be a blessed person, to live an abundant life, and to receive great things from Me. (See Luke 11:11–13.)
- I have given you a dream, a vision, and a hope. You are to live your life with your head lifted high, for you are Mine. (See Ephesians 1:11–12.)
- I love you the way you are, and I love you too much to let you stay the way you are. I am changing you for your good. (See Philippians 2:13.)

- I have chosen you. You are Mine. I want you. I will never reject you. You are forever Mine. (See John 10:27–29.)
- I have bought you with My blood. You are important. You are significant. You are special. (See Ephesians 1:7.)
- I have rescued you from the dark power of Satan's rule and have brought you into My kingdom. (See Colossians 1:13.)
- I have cleansed you. You are no longer impure and unrighteous. You are pure and holy. You are whole and beautiful. (See Hebrews 10:22.)

God's Thoughts toward You for a Full Life

In John 10:10, Jesus stated,

The thief does not come except to steal, and to kill, and to destroy. I have come that they may have life, and that they may have it more abundantly.

"The thief" is the enemy of your life and soul, the devil. He desires to steal from your life anything and everything that is good. He wants to hinder you from hearing God's thoughts toward you, and he wants to kill your dreams, your vision, your hope, and your faith. He wants to distort your perspective on life and destroy your attitude of faith for your future.

In contrast, Jesus said in the verse above that He came to bring abundant life. The psalmist said that a life lived in the presence of God is *"fullness of joy"* (Psalm 16:11). God wants to show you the path of life—the way of living that leads to a full and abundant life. This fullness of life comes from hearing God's thoughts toward you and living according to them. It comes from living in the presence of God and making choices in accordance with that lifestyle.

A full life is a life that is saturated, having more than enough. It is a life of surplus. God

> *God wants you to have a quality of life that is filled to overflowing, lacking nothing.*

wants you to have a quality of life that is filled to overflowing, lacking nothing. It is a life that is not limited or restricted, a life that is lived to its full completion and reaches its desired goals.

A full life is a life that experiences the good things of God. Psalm 16:6 says, *"My share in life has been pleasant; my part has been beautiful"* (NCV). Your heritage in God is one that is pleasant, lovely, satisfying, and long lasting. It is a life that receives the good things God has planned for you. (See Job 36:11.)

A full life is a life that is abundantly satisfied with God and His plans for you.

> *They are abundantly satisfied with the fullness of Your house, and You give them drink from the river of Your pleasures. For with You is the fountain of life; in Your light we see light.*
> (Psalm 36:8–9)

The full life is satisfied with the fullness and abundance that God has provided. The full life enjoys fullness in relationships, life principles, and wisdom for success. The full life drinks from the rivers of God's pleasures. These rivers are flowing streams of delight that are filled with the keys to living and enjoying a full life. In tumult and peace, both now and in the future, you can still enjoy all that God has provided and will continue to provide for your life.

Powerful God-Thoughts Produce Powerful God-Results

Isaiah 55:10–11 makes a powerful statement.

> *The rain and snow come down from the heavens and stay on the ground to water the earth. They cause the grain to grow, producing seed for the farmer and bread for the hungry. It is the same with my word. I send it out, and it always produces fruit. It will accomplish all I want it to, and it will prosper everywhere I send it.*
> (NLT)

God's promises will be fulfilled. Every word He has spoken will come to pass. Every purpose He has planned will be accomplished. That includes His thoughts and purposes for your life.

Open your mind to the thoughts of God toward you and believe that He will accomplish all He has purposed. Reach for His higher thoughts and His higher ways. (See Isaiah 55:9.) Do not settle for your limited thoughts, but aim for His higher thoughts. William Arthur Ward said, "Nothing limits achievement like small thinking. Nothing expands possibilities like unleashed thinking."[14]

Change your fear to faith. Change your doubt to belief. Believe God's thoughts toward you. Believe the promises in His Word. Poor thinking produces negative progress. Average thinking produces no progress. Good thinking produces some progress. Great thinking produces great progress. But God-thinking produces God-progress!

In the British Museum in London, there is a map of North America that was drawn in 1525. Parts of the map are incomplete, as those regions had not yet been explored by European cartographers. In those areas, the mapmaker had written, "Here be giants." "Here be fiery scorpions." "Here be dragons." Several hundred years later, a British explorer had gained possession of the map, had marked out those phrases, and had written in large letters, "Here is God."

On the map of your life, cross out the negative thoughts of fear and doubt and replace them with God's thoughts toward you. Cross out the words of limitation that others have spoken over your life and write, "Here is God." And with God, nothing is impossible.

Chapter 4

Yes to Kairos Living

A mother and daughter were driving along a narrow road in the mountains, enjoying the peaceful beauty of the tall evergreens that overshadowed the road. Rounding a corner, they suddenly broke out of the shaded world of the evergreens and into a panorama that shocked them into silence. They pulled their car over to the side of the road and sat gazing in amazement. A multicolored river of flowers swept down the mountainside in front of them. Sunlit daffodils and purple hyacinths streamed across the meadow as bold tulips and dancing bluebells splashed along the edges.

In the center of the river of flowers sat a small house on an island of green. Pushed by their curiosity, the mother and daughter got out of their car and began to wade through the field to find the owner of this amazing sight. As they approached the home, they saw a sign that read,

Answers to the questions I know you are asking:
1. One woman with two hands, two feet, and very little brain.
2. One at a time.
3. Started in 1958.

One woman changed her world. She did it one flower bulb at a time. It took her forty years, but she changed the face of that mountain. You have hopes for the future, expectations you would like to see become reality. What could you accomplish if you took one step each day? What could you grow if you planted one seed at a time? You can find out. All you have to do is start. Start today.

The Time Is Now

When is the right time to have great expectations for life and the future? Now. Today. Now is the time. Romans 15:13 says, *"Now may the God of hope fill you with all joy and peace in believing, that you may abound in hope by the power of the Holy Spirit."* Now—at this present time and moment. Now—under your present circumstances. Now—immediately and without delay.

> *Now is the time in your life to nurture great desires and expectations.*

Now is the time in your life to nurture great desires and expectations. Now is the day to renew those desires from the past that you have allowed to die. Remove the attitude of procrastination that does not expect anything good to happen today. Remove the attitude of delay that seeks to hinder your progress toward expectation.

The time for living your life with full and wonderful expectations is now. Whatever it takes, you need to avoid wasting precious time with a negative outlook and pessimistic thinking. Your attitude toward time has a profound impact on your life, your world, and your future. Wouldn't it be exciting if you could reclaim yesterday, enjoy today, and master tomorrow?

You must let go of the "poor me" mentality. The martyr complex hinders expectation for God to do something great for you now. No more excuses! Stop blaming life, blaming people, or blaming God. Stop rationalizing your inaction or feeling inadequate to live up to God's expectations. The time for a great expectation visitation in your life is now, at this present moment. Let go of the pessimistic attitude that expects the worst to happen.

The *now* moment of great God-expectations is upon you. Remove the indecision and move ahead. It is time to get off the fence. Now is the time to decide. You must know what to do and then do it. New horizons will be there if you get on with life. Lift your expectations today. Decide to pursue the vision, the dream, the goal. Make the decision that needs to be made. Every expectation comes to a decision. Decisions are the "go points" in life, the decisive moments when essential information has been gathered, the pros and cons have been weighed, and the time has come to act.

There was a group of teenage boys who enjoyed hopping trains for fun. As each train left the outskirts of town, it would slow down to round a curve. That was the "go point," the place at which the boys had one opportunity to jump off the train safely. Once that point had passed, the train quickly picked up speed and did not stop or slow down until it reached the next town. One young man missed the "go point." As his friends jumped, he stood vacillating from fear and indecision until the train picked up speed and disappeared into the distance. Several days later, he showed up at home with a hard-gained understanding of the necessity of acting when the time is right.

Now is that time. Today is your "go point." This is your door of opportunity to shape your destiny, to influence history, to move into something greater. Today is the day to begin to change the lives around you and influence businesses, institutions, and nations. This is your "go point." Act now!

The Now Factor of Expectation

Now is the time, you are the person, and God is your Source. *Expect* great and mighty things to happen to you and through you! In 2 Corinthians 6:2, God promised,

> *"In an acceptable time I have heard you, and in the day of salvation I have helped you." Behold, now is the accepted time; behold, now is the day of salvation.*

Time is your most valuable possession. Nothing you do in this life will allow you to accrue one extra minute of time, and nothing will allow you to regain time that has been mis-spent. When time is gone, it is gone forever.

In Scripture, there are two words to define and describe *time.* One word is *chronos,* which designates a period or space of time. It is close in meaning to the scientific way in which Westerners mark time using years, months, days, hours, minutes, and seconds.

> *Kairos designates the content and quality of time. It is a specific season, an opportune moment, or an appointed time.*

It is reflected in terms such as chronology, duration, clock, and calendar. The other word is *kairos*, which designates the content and the quality of the time. It is a noteworthy moment made significant by a divine encounter with God. It is a specific season, an opportune moment, or an appointed time.

Time is an important commodity. It is more important than money; it is your greatest and most important possession. Many people have financial advisers to assist them with investing their money. You have to become your own time investment planner, with God as your adviser, to learn how to invest your time wisely. Consider these questions carefully: *What do you want most out of life? How can you make every minute, hour, day, month, year, and decade matter?*

The person who believes in God and Scripture takes these questions to God and asks Him for His divine wisdom and direction. God knows your destiny and how to live life to fulfill that destiny. Your times are in His hands. Do not be satisfied with a time that simply marks days off the calendar, but expect a life that is lived in *kairos* time, a life that is lived with God-involvement and God-impact.

We must not live simply in *chronos* time but in *kairos* time. You can mark your life by days and hours, by months and years, or you can mark your life by *kairos* time, by the divine opportunities that you have embraced and by the God-encounters that are recorded in eternity. Without God, you will lose opportunities and waste the precious gift of time. Henry David Thoreau warned, "As if you could kill time without injuring eternity."[15] Do not waste your *kairos* opportunities. Value them. Treasure them. Psalm 90:12 says, "*Teach us to number our days, that we may gain a heart of wisdom.*"

The last words of Elizabeth I, Queen of England, were, "All my possessions for a moment of time." The apostle Paul summed up his life by saying, "*I have fought the good fight, I have finished the race, I have kept the faith. Finally, there is laid up for me the crown of righteousness"* (2 Timothy 4:7–8). How will you look back on your life? By begging for an extra *chronos* moment of time? Or by passionately declaring, "I have grasped every *kairos* moment and accomplished all that God had for me."

Like everything else in creation, time has been ordained by God, and it flows toward a determined future. It is marked by cycles and repetitions, yet it flows from a definite beginning to a predetermined culmination. We may find that personal experience intersects with appointed time ordained by God—and that will change the way we live. Our lives and times can be filled with *kairos* living and purpose. Our appointed times are in His hands and develop according to His purposes. As Psalm 102:13 says, *"You will arise and have mercy on Zion; for the time to favor her, yes, the set time, has come."*

Personal Testimony

Mike,
Business Owner in His Fifties

One seemingly small "Yes, Lord" can change your life in a very big way. In May 1982, I joined about one hundred people from the local church I was involved with to gather signatures for a petition to help stop tax-funded abortions in the State of Oregon. After spending a three-hour shift in a nearby mall, I turned in my signatures and began talking with the campaign coordinator.

Before the day was over, I had learned that the organization had very little money and only a small staff of volunteers to run their statewide campaign. After a short season of prayer and a conversation with my wife—a stay-at-home mother of one who also had to say yes to God—I quit my job as a warehouse manager and spent the next six months raising money and managing a heated political campaign.

For the next five years, I continued to serve as the first Executive Director of this pro-life organization. It grew from an annual income of approximately twenty-five thousand dollars per year to more than one million dollars. It's been twenty-eight years since my wife and I said yes to that divine prompting. Today, I still serve as the organization's finance director, but I also work with a host of other equally effective Christian charities and local churches who minister to orphans, on mission fields, and to the disadvantaged. I can't even imagine where my life would be had I said to God, "No, thanks."

Embracing Kairos Living

Kairos Living Recognizes the Divine Opportunities God Has Given You

God wants you to seize the moment when kairos opportunities cross your path.

Divine opportunities are favorable junctures of circumstances that God places into your life's journey. They are possibilities for great things to happen. God wants you to seize the moment when *kairos* opportunities cross your path. This is why you should redeem the time. (See Ephesians 5:16.) This is why you should expect divine opportunities to happen at the right times.

When the fullness of the time had come, God sent forth His Son, born of a woman, born under the law, to redeem those who were under the law, that we might receive the adoption as sons.
(Galatians 4:4–5)

Recognize your day of visitation and reach out to take hold of the divine opportunities. If you do not...

Your enemies will...level you, and your children within you, to the ground; and they will not leave in you one stone upon another, because you did not know the time of your visitation.
(Luke 19:43–44)

Kairos Living Personally Experiences the Appointed Times and Seasons God Has Given You

There are God-given moments in life that become eternal and mark you for eternity. Dedicating your life to God and giving yourself to serious prayer will allow you to intersect with the God-appointed events that God sends into your life.

Although everyone experiences God-appointed events, everyone does not necessarily make those events profitable. *Kairos* living responds to the God-given moments. Mark 1:15 says, *"The time is fulfilled, and the kingdom of God is at hand. Repent, and believe in the gospel."* Many heard the call of the God-appointed event, but only those who responded in repentance were marked for eternity. God has appointed seasons for you. These are times to expect God to fulfill His Word.

Kairos Living Is a Specific Season in Life When God-Ordained Events Happen to You

The word that Abraham and Sarah received about the miracle child coming to them, a supernatural opportunity and gift from God, is seen in Romans 9:9: *"For this is the word of promise: 'At this time I will come and Sarah shall have a son.'"* Scripture says *"at this time."* It was a fixed and definite time period when God would work a God-ordained miracle. It would be a time of fulfillment. Expectation would receive its reward.

Be encouraged and do not lose heart if the promises of God to you have been a long time in coming. Galatians 6:9 declares, *"Let us not grow weary while doing good, for in due season we shall reap if we do not lose heart."* You will reap in due season. Here, the *kairos* word is used again—*season.*

As God said to Abraham and Sarah in Genesis 18:14, *"Is anything too hard for the LORD? At the appointed time I will return to you, according to the time of life, and Sarah shall have a son."* Nothing is too hard for God at the appointed times in your life. Stop. Pray. Believe. Expect. You have the power through prayer to connect to heaven's throne, to cooperate with God's plan and purpose, to resist the devil, and to

> *You have the power through prayer to connect to heaven's throne, to cooperate with God's plan and purpose, to resist the devil, and to obtain God's promises.*

obtain God's promises. Move into your *kairos* season of life. This is the right time in your life to expect God to work powerfully.

Kairos Living Is Believing God's Words That Have Come into Your Life

God's Word can come into your life through reading the Bible, reaching into the Scriptures with an attitude of faith, and then pulling them back into your circumstances. The words of God can be quickened to you, made alive and personal as you declare them into your life and into your specific circumstances. God's Word can come to you through other people who have exhorted you, prayed for you, or given you prophetic insight. Believe the promises of Scripture:

Blessed be the LORD God of Israel, who spoke with His mouth to my father David, and with His hand has fulfilled it....You have kept what You promised Your servant David my father; You have both spoken with Your mouth and fulfilled it with Your hand, as it is this day. (1 Kings 8:15, 24)

Stand now and declare Psalm 20:4–5 over your life:

May He grant you according to your heart's desire, and fulfill all your purpose. We will rejoice in your salvation, and in the name of our God we will set up our banners! May the LORD fulfill all your petitions.

Stand in faith and believe Psalm 145:19:

He will fulfill the desire of those who fear Him; He also will hear their cry and save them.

Kairos Living Is a Time of Seeing the Full Favor of God on Your Life

Favor is the gracious kindness of God that lifts you to a place of respect, honor, and esteem because of His grace toward you. It places you at an advantage for success. According to the book of Acts, the members of the early church were…

> …*continuing daily with one accord in the temple, and breaking bread from house to house, they ate their food with gladness and simplicity of heart, praising God and having favor with all the people. And the Lord added to the church daily those who were being saved.* (Acts 2:46–47)

The favor of God is available in all situations. It comes in seasons of testing and in seasons of promotion. Favor provides a conviction that God is with you in every circumstance and causes you to keep doing your best whatever the situation—whether it is a place of setback or a place of success. God works with you and for you in every circumstance and place.

The favor of God is available in all situations. It comes in seasons of testing and in seasons of promotion.

This principle is seen in the life of Joseph. Genesis 39:21 says that "*the LORD was with Joseph,*" and he found favor—in testing and in promotion. In verses 3–4, Joseph found favor in the sight of his master, and God made everything he touched prosper. At the end of the chapter, Joseph ended up in prison, but still the Lord "*gave him favor in the sight of the keeper of the prison*" (verse 21).

You will find favor in the seasons of testing in your life. Those are the times that require maximum effort in difficult circumstances, yet even in those times, you will find favor. The grace of God will cover you, strengthen you, and bring you to a place of rest and assurance. His hand is on you even when the world seems like it is against you. He will not cast you aside, but He will fill you with His grace in that *kairos* season.

You will find favor in the seasons of promotion in your life. "*Humble yourselves under the mighty hand of God, that He may exalt you in due time*" (1 Peter 5:6). As you remain humble and faithful in the seasons of testing, God will bring seasons of promotion, and you will embrace that *kairos* time and step forth in the confidence of His leading and direction in your life.

Expect the favor of God in both your seasons of testing and your seasons of blessing. Expect the favor of God, and step into that *kairos* moment with confidence and boldness that God's hand is on your life. He will not leave you. He will lift you up.

What to Expect Now

Expect God to do in you everything He has promised in His Word. Have faith to receive those promises. Pray the following declaration now.

> In Jesus' name, by the power of the blood shed on the cross, by the authority of the Scriptures, I proclaim my life to be a blessed life both in my *now* and in my future. I proclaim blessing in all that pertains to my life: health, home, finances, and friends. I declare this time in my life to be a time of favor, blessing, new spiritual power, fresh Holy Spirit visitation, and great momentum.

Now is the time to expect God to break long-standing bondages that have hindered you from fulfilling your destiny.

The Holy Spirit seeks to invade your life and do a work in you now that will surpass anything in the past. Now, today, acknowledge the leadership of Christ in your life by giving Him the rightful place in the small and great areas alike. Now is the time to expect God to break long-standing bondages that have hindered you from fulfilling your destiny.

Malachi 3:2 warns, "*Who can endure the day of His coming? And who can stand when He appears? For He is like a refiner's fire and like launderers' soap.*" He is your refiner's fire. Do not resist, but fan the flames and let God burn up all the dead wood in your life.

> *His winnowing fan is in His hand, and He will thoroughly clean out His threshing floor, and gather His wheat into the barn; but He will burn up the chaff with unquenchable fire.*
> (Matthew 3:12)

Now is the time to become more sensitive to the voice of God in your life. John 10:3–4 says that Jesus is the Good Shepherd who *"calls his own sheep by name and leads them out. And when he brings out his own sheep, he goes before them; and the sheep follow him, for they know his voice."* Know the voice of Jesus. Listen to it daily until you become familiar with it and can recognize it instantly.

Still, it is not enough simply to know the Lord's voice. Hear God's voice and respond as Samuel did: "Here am I. What do you wish to say to me?"

> *The LORD called Samuel. And he answered, "Here I am!"…*
> *Now Samuel did not yet know the LORD, nor was the word of the LORD yet revealed to him….The LORD came and stood and called as at other times, "Samuel! Samuel!" And Samuel answered, "Speak, for Your servant hears."*
> (1 Samuel 3:4, 7, 10)

When you hear His voice and you respond, it begins to burn within you and ignite your spirit. In Luke 24, when the disciples were walking along the road to Emmaus, Jesus appeared and walked with them, but they did not recognize Him. They heard His words but did not recognize His physical voice. Still, Luke reports that their hearts responded to the voice of God speaking to their inner beings. In Luke 24:32, they asked each other, *"Did not our heart burn within us while He talked with us on the road, and while He opened the Scriptures to us?"*

The sound of His voice within their spirits kindled a fire that burned. The Scriptures say that God is a consuming fire (see Hebrews 12:29) and that we are to be baptized in the Holy Spirit and fire (see Matthew 3:11). God desires to remove all stagnation and lukewarmness from our lives. Lukewarmness is a condition of the soul that is content to remain neutral, fluctuating between hot and cold. It is a soul that lacks conviction and is uncommitted and indecisive.

Now is the time to expect change—to expect a new visitation of God upon your life to transform your lukewarmness into zeal and transform you from a cold Christian to one who is passionate and fired up. Now is the time to see and expect the vast possibilities that

God has set before you today and for your future. Believe that John 15:7 is for you: *"If you abide in Me, and My words abide in you, you will ask what you desire, and it shall be done for you."* Believe Mark 11:24: *"I say to you, whatever things you ask when you pray, believe that you receive them, and you will have them."*

> *Prayer enters into the impossible and opens new doors of possibilities.*

Prayer enters into the impossible and opens new doors of possibilities. The possibility of prayer reaches into the future and makes the future reality. Expect! Anything and everything becomes possible with prayer.

When will you remove the limits of your expectation? When will you stop limiting the word *whatsoever*? Whatever is left out of *whatsoever* is left out of prayer! Expect whatever you desire and pray in faith for it to become reality. *Now* is the time to lift your faith to accomplish great and mighty things through God.

> *Without faith it is impossible to please Him, for he who comes to God must believe that He is, and that He is a rewarder of those who diligently seek Him.* (Hebrews 11:6)

Great faith enables Christ to do great things. Matthew 21:22 promises, *"Whatever things you ask in prayer, believing, you will receive."* Inspire your heart to enlarge your prayers and reach for new possibilities. Prayer in its magnitude is length without end, width without bounds, height without top, and depth without bottom. It is the infinite without extension. Prayer is the story of great achievements.

> *Enlarge the place of your tent, and let them stretch out the curtains of your dwellings; do not spare; lengthen your cords, and strengthen your stakes.* (Isaiah 54:2)

Now is the time to expect great things from God and to pray great prayers to God. Expectation aims at specific and definite objects, seeking answers with focused dedication.

> *Ask, and it will be given to you; seek, and you will find; knock, and it will be opened to you....If you then, being evil, know how*

to give good gifts to your children, how much more will your
Father who is in heaven give good things to those who ask Him!
(Matthew 7:7, 11)

Consider the question God asked Solomon. *"At Gibeon the* LORD
appeared to Solomon in a dream by night; and God said, 'Ask! What shall I
give you?'" (1 Kings 3:5). If God asked you the same question, what
would you request?

"On that night God appeared to Solomon, and said to him, 'Ask! What
shall I give you?'" (2 Chronicles 1:7). If God gave you that choice,
what would your response be?

Now is the time to enlarge your view of God and see God's ability to do anything and everything He has promised. Now is the
time to make Matthew 19:26 a reality in your life: *"But Jesus looked*
at them and said to them, 'With men this is impossible, but with God all
things are possible.'"

Chapter 5

Yes to God as My Source

In the court of Alexander the Great, there was a scholar who excelled at philosophy but consistently failed at handling his finances properly. The story goes that one day, completely broke, he asked Alexander for financial help and was told to take whatever he needed from the imperial treasury. The man went to the treasurer and requested an amount equal to about fifty thousand dollars.

The treasurer was astonished. "Absolutely not! That is too much money. I want to hear from Alexander himself that you are authorized to get that much money." The treasurer went to Alexander the Great, sure that he would be told the philosopher should be refused, but Alexander replied, "Pay the money at once. The philosopher has done me a singular honor. By the largeness of his request, he shows that he has understood both my wealth and generosity."

Ask largely of God. He is not only a God who is able but also a God who is willing. Look to Him as the author and finisher of your expectation. Look to Him as the restorer of lost expectation. Pray the following prayer today.

> *Ask largely of God. He is not only a God who is able but also a God who is willing.*

Lord, today I lift up my eyes and my heart toward You, knowing where my help comes from. Lord, You are my wellspring of expectation. Today I place my faith firmly in the Word You have given me, the Scriptures, and in You, the God who is able to do exceedingly abundantly above all that I can ask or think. You are watching over my life, and I put my expectations in Your hands. I believe and embrace Romans 15:13: *"May the God of hope fill you with all joy and peace in believing, that you may abound in hope by the power of the Holy Spirit."* Amen.

The philosopher from Alexander's court knew the ruler with whom he was dealing. He knew that Alexander was a generous man who *would* supply the money, and he also knew that Alexander had the *ability* to supply it. He knew his ruler, so he expected largely.

You are to be a person who abounds with hope and expectation. You are to be full of this precious spiritual virtue—expectation—and you can expect largely only if you know the One from whom you are expecting to receive. There can be no true, well-founded, far-reaching hope that is not fixed on the God of hope, on His providential power and rule, on His gracious purposes, and on His trustworthy, never-changing, never-failing promises.

God inspires expectation. God rewards expectation. He is the God who supplies your heart and life with an overflow of expectation. Psalm 62:5 says, *"God, the one and only—I'll wait as long as he says. Everything I hope for comes from him, so why not?"* (MSG).

The Source of Expectation Is a Right Perspective on God

God the Promisor, the true God revealed in Scriptures, is the God we believe in and put our faith in. It is interesting how much information there is on the Internet about finding and knowing God. In early 2009, an Internet search for pages related to God returned over sixty-four million results—more than most other common topics. Browsing through some of these pages revealed that different people have very different understandings of who God is and what their relationships with Him should be like.

Everything about your life—attitudes, motives, desires, actions, and expectations—are influenced by your vision and your understanding of God. Some misconceptions will hinder your relationship with God and ultimately your expectations of God in your life.

In their book *Relationships*, Drs. Les and Leslie Parrott give four misconceptions that people can have about God.

The Referee God. Some people see God as a referee who tallies points for good performance on a huge scoreboard in the sky. These people are consumed by religious rules and the fear that they will step out of line and suffer a penalty. They may get away with a few fouls or errors when God isn't looking, but most of the time these poor people are motivated by guilt and obsessed with avoiding God's wrath.

The Grandfather God. Many people use their interpretation of God to keep them from growing up—to avoid responsibility. And by viewing God as a warm grandfatherly figure, they remain a child. They want to be told, "There's nothing to worry about; I'll take care of everything for you."

The Scientist God. A "superior reasoning power," is how Einstein conceptualized God. "A superior mind," is how he said it on another occasion. For some, God is a withdrawn and distant thinker, too busy running the galaxies to get involved in our petty problems. God is sitting in his laboratory, conducting experiments with his door closed and a "Do Not Disturb" sign on it.

The Bodyguard God. Some people think of God much the same way a sailor thinks of a lifeboat. He knows it is there, but he hopes he'll never have to use it. These people live life without giving much conscious attention to God, but they expect him to be there when they need him. When we view God this way, we believe he should serve as a kind of bodyguard to protect us from pain and suffering. "If I'm living a good life," so the reasoning goes, "then God should look after me and keep me out of harm's way."[16]

You will expect from God in direct proportion to your knowledge of and relationship with Him.

So, who is the God who is the source of your expectations? What is He like? What is His nature? You will expect from God in direct proportion to your knowledge of and relationship with Him.

Personal Testimony

Derrill,
Senior Pastor of Life Center in Centralia, Washington;
In His Thirties; Began Pastoring in His Twenties

In order to say yes to God as my Source, I have found it necessary to say no to the enemy as the one who tries to devour! During a season of great challenge, our church faced what seemed to be an immovable mountain. Over a ten-year period of time, we had developed and renovated a run-down warehouse in a depressed area of our city. The facility had really become a beautiful statement of God's provision, as a faith-filled people were persistent and faithful with what He entrusted to us. People were amazed as they entered the doors of our building, and we were thrilled with what God had provided for us.

Being woken up in the middle of the night by one of our staff members calling to say that the building was flooded with around three feet of water was not something my wife and I ever expected. Basically, the result of ten years of blood, sweat, and tears was wiped away in a matter of hours. The degree of loss we felt cannot be described in words. Questions ran through our minds, such as, *Will the church survive? What about our stuff? How will we pay our employees?*

Within a matter of hours, something rose up inside of both of us that said, *No! The enemy will not stop what God has begun!* We quickly began to proclaim the breadth of the Word of God over our church, to our own spirits, and to the one who would try to devour. The Lord began to supernaturally bring in funds from all over the world. Thousands of dollars poured in, and within one week, we had the flooded facility cleaned up, a new place to meet secured, and our direction set. The Holy Spirit began to inspire a fresh sense of His presence in our worship and prayer times, and the people rallied around the dream.

Paralleled with this tragedy was a downturn in our national economy. These two crises at one time could have potentially shut down our entire work of faith. As we kept saying yes to God and no to the enemy, the provision has been there. We ended our year on budget and have now turned our old flooded building into a community out-reach facility called The City of Refuge. It has become an arm of the church, and we minister through this neighbor-hood family resource center to the hurting and the lost in a depressed area.

God continues to provide, and we see His hand in opera-tion every day. I can truly say that we must all say yes to God as our Source. Unless He builds the house, all our labor is in vain.

Yes to the Sovereign God Who Made You

Basic Christian doctrine states that there is one God who is sovereign. While He is transcendent and beyond us, He is also immanent, right here among us. He cre-ated everything—the universe, the world in which we live. Furthermore, He did it with absolutely nothing. He did not rear-range or put together matter of some kind. He created everything from nothing.

You are God's crowning creation. God spoke at creation, and a complex, wonder-ful universe came into being. Genesis 2:7 says that when God made man, He didn't just speak—He *"breathed into his nostrils the breath of life; and man became a living being."*

God breathed His own breath into man. He breathed into us the ability to reason, the capacity to understand, and the aptitude for creativity.

God breathed His own breath into man. Nothing else has the breath of God—only man. He breathed into us the ability to reason, the capacity to understand, and the aptitude for creativity. He made us in His own image. We are spirit beings.

You are made in God's image. When you die, you will either go to be with Him or be separated from Him forever. There will be no coming back to try to get it right the second time. Because sin prevents you from getting it right in the first place, God sent His Son, part of Himself, to redeem you and justify you. Christ died for your sins according to the Scriptures. He was buried. He rose from the dead on the third day, as the Scripture said would happen, and He is alive now.

This is the message upon which your expectations are built. It is given by God—the only true and powerful God, who is personally involved in your life. He speaks to you. He communes with you. And He has a plan and purpose for you.

Yes to the Greatness of God

The God who makes promises to us and in whom we place our trust and expectation is a great God. We can and should believe that He can bring our hopes, dreams, and expectations to fulfillment.

For since the creation of the world His invisible attributes are clearly seen, being understood by the things that are made, even His eternal power and Godhead, so that they are without excuse.
(Romans 1:20)

The heavens declare the glory of God; the skies proclaim the work of his hands. Day after day they pour forth speech; night after night they display knowledge. There is no speech or language where their voice is not heard. Their voice goes out into all the earth, their words to the ends of the world.
(Psalm 19:1–4 NIV)

Bill Bright describes the message of creation in his book *God: Discover His Character.*

To get just a small idea of God's creative power, let us consider our universe. We live on one of nine planets that revolve around the sun. As the dominant light of our solar system, our sun gives off far more energy in one second than all mankind has produced since creation. With a diameter of approximately 860,000 miles, the sun could hold one million planets the size of the Earth, yet our sun is only an average-size star.

Our sun is just one among 100 billion stars in our galaxy, the Milky Way. The Pistol Star gives off 10 million times the power generated by our sun, and one million stars the size of our sun can fit easily within its sphere. It takes 100,000 light-years to travel from one side of the Milky Way to the other. (One light-year is 5.88 trillion miles or the distance light travels in one year.) Our galaxy is moving through space at a phenomenal speed of one million miles per hour! If the Milky Way were compared to the size of the North American continent, our solar system would be about the size of a coffee cup!

Yet our Milky Way is not a huge galaxy. One of our neighbors, the Andromeda Spiral galaxy, is two million light-years away and contains about 400 billion stars. No one knows how many galaxies there are in the universe, but scientists estimate that there are billions of them....Scientists estimate that there are ten billion trillion stars in the universe, or about as many stars as there are grains of sand on all of our planet's seashores. If all the stars were divided equally among the people of the world, each person would receive almost two trillion stars![17]

The prophets Jeremiah and Isaiah marveled in amazement.

Ah, Sovereign Lord, you have made the heavens and the earth by your great power and outstretched arm. Nothing is too hard for you. You show love to thousands but bring the punishment for the fathers' sins into the laps of their children after them. O great and powerful God, whose name is the

LORD Almighty, great are your purposes and mighty are your deeds. Your eyes are open to all the ways of men; you reward everyone according to his conduct and as his deeds deserve.
(Jeremiah 32:17–19 NIV)

Look up into the heavens. Who created all the stars? He brings them out like an army, one after another, calling each by its name. Because of his great power and incomparable strength, not a single one is missing.   (Isaiah 40:26 NLT)

The psalmist proclaimed,

By the word of the LORD the heavens were made, and all the host of them by the breath of His mouth. He gathers the waters of the sea together as a heap; He lays up the deep in storehouses. Let all the earth fear the LORD; let all the inhabitants of the world stand in awe of Him. For He spoke, and it was done; He commanded, and it stood fast. The LORD brings the counsel of the nations to nothing; He makes the plans of the peoples of no effect. The counsel of the LORD stands forever, the plans of His heart to all generations.
(Psalm 33:6–11)

Genesis 1:26 tells us that God made man in His own image and according to His likeness. Man is a mirror or reflection of God in his capacity to think, imagine, feel, act with freedom, and understand right and wrong. The man God created is a marvelous and wonderful creation. The psalmist expounded on this truth, saying,

For You formed my inward parts; You covered me in my mother's womb. I will praise You, for I am fearfully and wonderfully made; marvelous are Your works, and that my soul knows very well. My frame was not hidden from You, when I was made in secret, and skillfully wrought in the lowest parts of the earth. Your eyes saw my substance, being yet unformed. And in Your book they all were written, the days fashioned for me, when as yet there were none of them.   (Psalm 139:13–16)

Again, let us look at Bill Bright's description of the workmanship of God in designing us. This is a design that God put into place at the moment of conception and will keep working out in us until our final breaths.

Let us think for a moment about what God sustains for each of us. It is estimated that as adults our bodies contain 60 trillion cells that have all been carefully organized to perform life's various functions in harmony. Consider these other facts about the human body: Our noses can recognize up to 10,000 different aromas. Our tongues have about 6,000 taste buds. Our brains contain ten billion nerve cells. Each brain nerve cell is connected to as many as 10,000 other nerve cells throughout the body. Our body has so many blood vessels that their combined length could circle the planet two-and-a-half times.

God also customized each of us with our own special DNA blueprint, which is contained within every single cell. It has been estimated that if your individual blueprint was written out in a book, it would require 200,000 pages. And God knows every word on every page![18]

We love and serve a God who has revealed Himself to be the only true God, a God with a defined nature, and a God with attributes and characteristics that you and I can know and love. The greatest need in our lives today is to discover the true identity of God and put our trust in Him.

Our expectations are only as good as the person in whom we place them. We have a choice. We can oppose the only true God and build an unstable life without God or belief in Him. We can build our lives on false human conceptions of God or on the way that philosophers and writers make Him out to be, or we can build our lives on who God shows Himself to be. Let God show you who He is, what He is like, and what He can do for you.

Our expectations are only as good as the person in whom we place them.

Yes to the Omnipotent God

God is omnipotent (all-powerful) and mighty. He is unlimited and infinite. We are finite, confined to space and time. God has no confinement and no limitations. He is high and lifted up, exalted above everything earthly and human. Psalm 147:5 proclaims, *"Great is our Lord, and mighty in power; His understanding is infinite."*

The God we expect to do great and mighty things is the God of all power, unlimited authority, and influence. God never has to ask permission. He is unrestrained, indescribable, and infinite in power; His abilities have no parameters.

> *The LORD reigns, He is clothed with majesty; the LORD is clothed, He has girded Himself with strength. Surely the world is established, so that it cannot be moved.* (Psalm 93:1)

God has boundless sufficiency. (See Genesis 17:1, 28:3; Psalm 91:1; Revelation 1:8, 9:8.) God is mighty and all-powerful, and He wields great command. (See Genesis 49:24; Deuteronomy 4:37, 9:29; Nehemiah 9:32; Psalm 24:8; Ephesians 1:19.) God is powerful, possessing and exerting great force with great effect. (See Psalm 29:4; Exodus 15:6; 1 Chronicles 29:1; Psalm 59:16; Matthew 6:13.) God is great, vast, extensive, wonderful, superior, and preeminent. (See Deuteronomy 7:21; Nehemiah 1:5, 4:14, 8:6; Psalm 77:8, 56:10.)

God is supreme—the highest in authority. He has no bounds or restrictions but is mighty in His works and powerful in His achievements. Without effort, God can do whatever He wills. He is the highest power, and nothing is too difficult for Him to accomplish or beyond His capacity. God is the God of omnipotence, both in actuality and in possibility. There are no limitations with God.

What this means for you is that God's will is never frustrated. What He chooses to do, He accomplishes. He has the ability to do it, and He has the resources to do it. Your expectations are in this God of power. Why would you not expect great things from a great God who has great power to accomplish all the great things you could ever conceive?

Yes to the Personal God Who Cares for Me

Any view of God that sees Him as an impersonal idea, or perhaps as some principle or law on which man is based, is not an accurate understanding of the nature of God. God is intimately involved with His people, not distant and uninterested.

> *You formed my inward parts; You covered me in my mother's womb. I will praise You, for I am fearfully and wonderfully made; marvelous are Your works, and that my soul knows very well.*
> (Psalm 139:13–14)

Any view of God that sees Him as an impersonal idea, or perhaps as some principle or law on which man is based, is not an accurate understanding of the nature of God.

The God of Scripture is one who thinks, feels, wills, laughs, and rejoices with His people. He feels sorrow and pain with His people. God loves you and will meet the deepest needs of Your life. He watches over you, strategizing for your good throughout the events of life.

Expectation is founded on a rock, a firm place—God. God is not some impersonal energy. He is actively involved in your life, and He is never indifferent, cold, or uninterested. In Job 29:2, Job reflected back on his life: *"Oh, that I were as in months past, as in the days when God watched over me."* God promises,

> *Because he has set his love upon Me, therefore I will deliver him; I will set him on high, because he has known My name. He shall call upon Me, and I will answer him; I will be with him in trouble; I will deliver him and honor him.* (Psalm 91:14–15)

God cares. He watches over you and prepares your future. He guides your steps so that nothing is left to chance or fate. He is in absolute control, and nothing that happens in your life catches God by surprise.

To God, you are not just a number, a faceless name, or a cog in the machine of humanity. You are very important to Him.

The LORD your God in your midst, the Mighty One, will
save; He will rejoice over you with gladness, He will quiet
you with His love, He will rejoice over you with singing.
(Zephaniah 3:17)

Everything about you and your future is important to Him.
You can trust Him totally. You can declare with the psalmist, "*The*
LORD is my rock and my fortress and my deliverer; my God, my strength,
in whom I will trust; my shield and the horn of my salvation, my strong-
hold" (Psalm 18:2).

Yes to the Unfailing Promises of God

God is the Promisor, and His Word can never fail, so you can
have great expectation in Him. In Psalm 123:1, the psalmist declares,
"*Unto You I lift up my eyes, O You who dwell in the heavens.*" Psalm
119:89 proclaims, "*Forever, O LORD, Your word is settled in heaven.*"

A promisor is the one who pledges to another to do or not to do
something specified. A declaration gives the person to whom the
promise is made the right to expect or claim the forbearance or performance of the specified promise. The promise is a pledge, a word
of honor, a vow, an oath, a warranty, a guarantee, or a covenant. It
is the ground of hope, expectation, assurance, and eventual achievement. God fulfills the promises He makes to us. Numbers 23:19
forcefully declares,

God is not a man, that He should lie, nor a son of man, that
He should repent. Has He said, and will He not do? Or has He
spoken, and will He not make it good?

If God makes a promise, His very nature will not allow Him to
leave it unfulfilled. And the promises He gives us are good ones. In
Psalm 37:4, He promises, "*Delight yourself also in the LORD, and He shall*
give you the desires of your heart." And in Matthew 7:8, He promises,
"*For everyone who asks receives, and he who seeks finds, and to him who*
knocks it will be opened."

God secures His promises with His character. It is impossible for
God to fail to keep His word. It is His nature and character, and He

cannot do otherwise. The author of Hebrews repeated the declaration of Numbers 23:19:

> *God secures His promises with His character. It is impossible for God to fail to keep His word.*

...that by two immutable things, in which it is impossible for God to lie, we might have strong consolation, who have fled for refuge to lay hold of the hope set before us.
(Hebrews 6:18)

God guards the promises He gives to us. In Jeremiah 1:12, He declared to Jeremiah, *"You have seen well, for I am ready to perform My word."* When King Solomon gave his dedication speech for the temple, he stood before the people of Israel and stated,

> *Blessed be the LORD, who has given rest to His people Israel, according to all that He promised. There has not failed one word of all His good promise, which He promised through His servant Moses.*
> (1 Kings 8:56)

God accomplishes His promised purposes for us.

> *For as the rain comes down, and the snow from heaven, and do not return there, but water the earth, and make it bring forth and bud, that it may give seed to the sower and bread to the eater, so shall My word be that goes forth from My mouth; it shall not return to Me void, but it shall accomplish what I please, and it shall prosper in the thing for which I sent it.*
> (Isaiah 55:10–11)

When rain leaves the clouds and falls onto the earth, it does not stop in midair and go back to the clouds. It continues down and fulfills its purpose. In the same way, when God sends His Word to accomplish something, it will not come back to Him but will go and fulfill His purpose.

God supplies whatever is needed for the promise. When God makes a promise, He does not leave it up to us to make that promise happen. If He makes a promise, He gives all that is necessary to see that promise fulfilled. In Genesis 17, God made a covenant

100 • *The Attitude of Faith*

with Abraham and promised him that he would be "*a father of many nations*" (verse 4). He did not leave it in Abraham's hands to figure out how to make that happen, but He visited Abraham and Sarah and caused them to have a son—the seed that was promised.

God finishes the promises He invests in us. God does not just start out with the promises. He brings them all the way through to completion. He does not get us halfway there and then stop, but He goes through to the end. Hebrews 10:23 tells us to "*hold fast the confession of our hope without wavering, for He who promised is faithful.*" Hold on to the promise, because He is faithful.

God enriches our lives with His steadfast promises. They are promises we can depend on—promises of blessing and good things for our lives. Psalm 67:6 promises, "*Then the earth shall yield her increase; God, our own God, shall bless us.*" In Psalm 84:11 we read, "*The LORD God is a sun and shield; the LORD will give grace and glory; no good thing will He withhold from those who walk uprightly.*" He will not hold back the good things but will pour abundant blessings on those who walk after Him.

> *The reflection of God's character is a just and glorious testimony to God's reliability.*

A saying in the world today goes, "Promises are like premade pie crusts—lightly made and easily broken." But the reflection of God's character is a just and glorious testimony to God's reliability. God is rich and abundant in His promises. He is very clear in what He has said.

Say yes to God's promises. Believe. Expect. Lift your hopes. "*For all the promises of God in Him are Yes, and in Him Amen, to the glory of God through us*" (2 Corinthians 1:20). God's promises are concrete and unmistakable. His deeds match His declarations. His divine promises cannot fail. He is the God of the universe, and all His laws are under His control and command. Nothing can stand in the way of the fulfillment of any promise He has made. Omnipotence is His. He can never, on any ground of incapacity, default on any promise.

God is trustworthy. (See Numbers 23:19; Psalm 18:20, 119:42.) God never lies. (See Hebrews 6:18; Psalm 119:160; James 1:17.)

God is faithful. (See Hebrews 10:23; Lamentations 3:23.) God is able to fulfill His Word. (See 1 Kings 8:56; Isaiah 55:10–11.)

The Expectation Promises

God has given us definite promises upon which we can stand. He promised ultimate victory in the very beginning.

> *I will put enmity between you and the woman, and between your seed and her Seed; He shall bruise your head, and you shall bruise His heel.* (Genesis 3:15)

Paul referred to this in Romans 16:20 when he wrote, "*The God of peace will crush Satan under your feet shortly.*"

God has promised blessings upon His people. The psalmist declared, "*Then the earth shall yield her increase; God, our own God, shall bless us*" (Psalm 67:6).

> *All these blessings shall come upon you and overtake you, because you obey the voice of the* LORD *your God....The* LORD *will command the blessing on you in your storehouses and in all to which you set your hand, and He will bless you in the land which the* LORD *your God is giving you.* (Deuteronomy 28:2, 8)

God has promised that His divine presence will be with us. Hebrews 13:5 says, "*I will never leave you nor forsake you,*" a promise this is repeated in Matthew 28:20, which reads, "*I am with you always, even to the end of the age.*" When His presence is with us, we can have confidence and trust because He is there.

> *When you pass through the waters, I will be with you; and through the rivers, they shall not overflow you. When you walk through the fire, you shall not be burned, nor shall the flame scorch you.* (Isaiah 43:2)

God's presence in our lives leads to the promise of peace in times of storm. Colossians 3:15 says, "*Let the peace of God rule in your hearts, to which also you were called in one body; and be thankful.*"

The promise of healing is seen in Psalm 103:2–3: *"Bless the LORD, O my soul, and forget not all His benefits: Who forgives all your iniquities, Who heals all your diseases,"* and in Exodus 15:26: *"I will put none of the diseases on you which I have brought on the Egyptians. For I am the LORD who heals you."*

God also promises His divine protection. In Zechariah 2:5, God promised, *"I…will be a wall of fire all around her, and I will be the glory in her midst."* In Psalm 61:2, David exulted, *"From the end of the earth I will cry to You, when my heart is overwhelmed; lead me to the rock that is higher than I."* (See also Psalm 57:1; Isaiah 32:2.)

God promises abundant provision. Philippians 4:19 states, *"My God shall supply all your need according to His riches in glory by Christ Jesus."* The limit of His provision is His unlimited riches! Psalm 84:11 tells us, *"For the LORD God is a sun and shield; the LORD will give grace and glory; no good thing will He withhold from those who walk uprightly."*

In the book of James, we find God's promise of wisdom. When you find yourself in situations where you do not know what to do, you can expect that God will hear when you ask. You can expect that God will give you His wisdom.

> *If any of you lacks wisdom, let him ask of God, who gives to all liberally and without reproach, and it will be given to him. But let him ask in faith, with no doubting, for he who doubts is like a wave of the sea driven and tossed by the wind.*
> (James 1:5–6)

God has promised that the Holy Spirit will help us. Jesus referred to the Holy Spirit when He promised,

> *If you then, being evil, know how to give good gifts to your children, how much more will your Father who is in heaven give good things to those who ask Him!* (Matthew 7:11)

Later, Jesus repeated this promise to the disciples in the gospel of John. (See also Ephesians 1:14; Acts 2:39, 1:4.)

> *And I will pray the Father, and He will give you another Helper, that He may abide with you forever.…But the Helper, the Holy*

Spirit, whom the Father will send in My name, He will teach you all things, and bring to your remembrance all things that I said to you. (John 14:16, 26)

Finally, God has promised us that He will give us sufficient grace for every situation in life.

Lest I should be exalted above measure by the abundance of the revelations, a thorn in the flesh was given to me, a messenger of Satan to buffet me, lest I be exalted above measure. Concerning this thing I pleaded with the Lord three times that it might depart from me. And He said to me, "My grace is sufficient for you, for My strength is made perfect in weakness." Therefore most gladly I will rather boast in my infirmities, that the power of Christ may rest upon me. (2 Corinthians 12:7–9)

Many are the afflictions of the righteous, but the LORD delivers him out of them all. (Psalm 34:19)

Chapter 6

Yes to Breakthrough

Breakthroughs often take people by surprise. They are part of life's rare happenings, arising out of a combination of God-engineered events in our lives. They are called *breakthroughs* because they do something that most people do not realize is possible. A breakthroughs creates something new and satisfies a previously undiscovered need. Breakthroughs in the business realm can launch new industries or transition existing ones. Breakthroughs in your personal life can open new doors and take your life to a new level, increasing your excitement for living.

Breakthrough is a place of new birth and new beginnings. It is a place of breaking forth with sudden force, breaking out of a restraining condition and advancing into a new area of life. Are you ready for some breakthroughs in your life, job, family, business, or church? God desires for you to rise to new challenges and new horizons, take new ground, and learn to live a life you love.

When you say *yes* to breakthrough, you are saying *yes* to removing any and all long-standing obstacles so that you can advance to a new level in God and life and enter into new opportunities. You are choosing to allow God to break through for you—and in you—so that you can go beyond any previous limitations.

> *When you say yes to breakthrough, you are saying yes to removing any and all long-standing obstacles.*

When you cooperate with God and His principles of breakthrough, you create consistent and practical spiritual breakthroughs in every area of life. You may need to acknowledge and lovingly confront issues that demand attention. In so doing, you release those issues, creating an opening for greater breakthroughs in your life. Everyone needs serious decision breakthroughs, circumstance breakthroughs, new opportunity breakthroughs, financial release breakthroughs, business blessing breakthroughs, and healing recovery breakthroughs.

Saying yes to breakthroughs takes you to a position of faith and expectation in the power of God, who is able to do the impossible. God wants to bring you into a place where you will find the breakthrough you need. Our God is the gate-crashing, wall-breaking, obstacle-removing God. He will open up any door He has ordered you to go through, even if it seems to be blocked. God is the battering ram who breaks open the door and makes a way where there is no way.

Look at Micah 2:13 in the following two translations:

Someone will open the way and lead the people out. The people will break through the gate and leave the city where they were held captive. Their king will go out in front of them, and the LORD will lead them. (NCV)

Then I, God, will burst all confinements and lead them out into the open. They'll follow their King. I will be out in front leading them. (MSG)

A *breakthrough* person looks at an obstacle of any size as a place for miracles to be received and for new achievements to take place. This *breakthrough* attitude of faith believes that God has great things in store for you and that you will not be defeated by the challenges that confront you.

The Hebrew word for *breakthrough* is *mishber*, which is the concept of an offensive move that goes beyond a defensive line in warfare. It is an act or instance of breaking through an obstacle with a sudden advance into a new area. Other words used for *breakthrough* are *shatter, break up, crush, burst, break in pieces, demolish, overthrow, advance, divide,* and *go forward.*

The *breakthrough* person has a faith focus that stretches toward the challenge and refuses to draw back. In the Bible, Joshua exemplified this attitude.

> *Then the LORD said to Joshua, "Stretch out the spear that is in your hand toward Ai, for I will give it into your hand." And Joshua stretched out the spear that was in his hand toward the city....For Joshua did not draw back his hand, with which he stretched out the spear, until he had utterly destroyed all the inhabitants of Ai.* (Joshua 8:18, 26)

Joshua did not waver, he did not lose faith, and he did not give up. He stood steadfastly in obedience to what God had said and saw a complete victory.

Christ Is the Breaker

The term *breaker,* as used in connection with Christ, may be foreign to some people. Scripture calls Christ the "Breaker," and "breakthrough" is one of the titles that describes His work in our lives. See God as one who is breaking through for you, conquering and leading the victors through the gate!

> *The one who breaks open will come up before them; they will break out, pass through the gate, and go out by it; their king will pass before them, with the LORD at their head.* (Micah 2:13)

See God as one who is breaking through for you, conquering and leading the victors through the gate!

Something has to be given to people so they can break through. Someone has to lead the way into breakthrough. In the book of Micah, the prophet prophesied that the Breaker would crash through the gates in order to lead the people into new, open places, much like a shepherd breaks open or clears the way for his sheep, going before them and leading them out the gate into the pasture.

In the same way, the Lord will remove all obstacles to blessing for His people. He will not abandon you in the hard times. He is the Jehovah-Messiah, the one who breaks through every obstacle that stands in the way before you. He is all-powerful. Nothing can resist or withstand His power. He clears the road for you to travel toward your destiny.

Christ is your anointed King. He is Jehovah. He goes before you as the captain and the Lord of hosts. Christ is the Breaker-Messiah, or the Breaker anointing, as seen in Isaiah.

> *It shall come to pass in that day that his burden will be taken away from your shoulder, and his yoke from your neck, and the yoke will be destroyed because of the anointing oil.*
> (Isaiah 10:27)

It is through His anointing that you have the freedom to fulfill your purpose.

> *God anointed Jesus of Nazareth with the Holy Spirit and with power, who went about doing good and healing all who were oppressed by the devil, for God was with Him.* (Acts 10:38)

Isaiah also says that Christ breaks through every obstacle and leads the captives out into new freedom.

> *I, the LORD, have called You in righteousness, and will hold Your hand; I will keep You and give You as a covenant to the people, as a light to the Gentiles, to open blind eyes, to bring out prisoners from the prison, those who sit in darkness from the prison house.* (Isaiah 42:6–7)

Nothing can hold you back when Christ calls you forth into your breakthrough. Again, in the book of Isaiah, God declares,

> *I will say to the north, "Give them up!" And to the south, "Do not keep them back!" Bring My sons from afar, and My daughters from the ends of the earth.* (Isaiah 43:6)

The Breaker leads His anointed people into breakthrough experiences.

The Breakthrough Anointing Is upon You

The Holy Spirit, whom Christ has given us, is the Breaker anointing.

Now He who establishes us with you in Christ and has anointed us is God, who also has sealed us and given us the Spirit in our hearts as a guarantee. (2 Corinthians 1:21–22)

You must be passionately seeking the fullness of the Holy Spirit, desiring it to fill you, expand your soul, enlarge your heart, extend your reach, and flow into you and out from you like a mighty river. Receive the abundant overflow of the anointing given by the Holy Spirit into your life, resulting in more of Jesus and a new, powerful breakthrough anointing.

Lead me in Your truth and teach me, for You are the God of my salvation; on You I wait all the day. (Psalm 25:5)

You love righteousness and hate wickedness; therefore God, Your God, has anointed You with the oil of gladness more than Your companions. (Psalm 45:7)

God desires to anoint you with this Breaker anointing now and every day. He desires to anoint you with fresh oil from on high, as in Psalm 92:10: *"My horn You have exalted like a wild ox; I have been anointed with fresh oil."*

The anointing of the Holy Spirit is the seal of God on your life. Biblically, the seal was a proof of authenticity. The royal seal of the king proved his authority and power and was an official mark of ownership and confirmation. You are a candidate for the Breaker anointing upon your life. Ask. Receive. Respond eagerly and step into the place where God is at work for you. Seize the opportunity to enter new gates.

> *The anointing of the Holy Spirit is the seal of God on your life.*

We must be born of the Spirit, who becomes our entrance into the kingdom of God. Jesus said,

Most assuredly, I say to you, unless one is born of water and the Spirit, he cannot enter the kingdom of God. That which is born of the flesh is flesh, and that which is born of the Spirit is spirit.
(John 3:5–6)

This was reiterated by Paul in 1 Corinthians 6:17: *"He who is joined to the Lord is one spirit with Him."*

We are to be baptized in the Holy Spirit:

John answered, saying to all, "I indeed baptize you with water; but One mightier than I is coming, whose sandal strap I am not worthy to loose. He will baptize you with the Holy Spirit and fire."
(Luke 3:16)

John truly baptized with water, but you shall be baptized with the Holy Spirit not many days from now.   (Acts 1:5)

Ephesians tells us that we are to be continually filled with the Holy Spirit—an ongoing experience of being filled with the anointing. It is not a one-time command; we should keep on being filled.

Do not be drunk with wine, in which is dissipation; but be filled with the Spirit, speaking to one another in psalms and hymns and spiritual songs, singing and making melody in your heart to the Lord.   (Ephesians 5:18–19)

> *The anointing upon you is a transfer of authority, power, and honor.*

The New Testament anointing is a spiritual empowering or outpouring of the Holy Spirit upon you, the blood-washed believer, that consecrates you to God and equips you with the Holy Spirit. The anointing is the power and influence in your life that permeates and saturates who you are, what you say, and what you do in service to the Lord. The anointing upon you is a divine enabler that goes beyond your own capacity, beyond your own strength, and beyond your own vision of the future. It is a transfer of authority, power, and honor.

The Breaker anointing is a divine influence upon your human faculties, human failures, human weaknesses, and human ineffectiveness. It is the power of God in action—the strength and might of God to take dominion over the enemy and to exercise the authority of Christ to establish God's rule and build His church.

The Breaker Anointing Is upon You to Break You into New Seasons in Your Life

The Breaker anointing upon you is the power of God in you and through you that breaks through every challenge you face in every season of life. We all have seasons of life—times of change because of particular circumstances, special opportunities, and specific challenges, crises, successes, or failures. They are seasons that come and go, each one leaving its mark upon us.

Ecclesiastes 3:1 says, *"To everything there is a season, a time for every purpose under heaven."* Each season of life has a unique challenge requiring breakthrough in an area that has not been conquered in the past. Galatians 6:9 promises, *"And let us not grow weary while doing good, for in due season we shall reap if we do not lose heart."*

In 1962, Victor and Mildred Goertzel published their research of four hundred famous twentieth century men and women to describe what common factors could be found in their lives. They found that three-quarters of these eminent men and women came from childhoods that were troubled by poverty, broken homes, poor parenting, financial difficulties, physical handicaps, or parental disapproval. One hundred of these four hundred suffered from handicaps, such as being blind, deaf, crippled, sickly, homely, undersized, overweight, or having speech defects. Yet none of these people succumbed to the difficulties in his or her life; all of these people used those difficulties to catapult them into becoming people of influence in the world.

In the natural, we have four seasons: spring, summer, fall, and winter. In the journey of life, we also pass through seasons of joy, tribulations, successes, and failures. You can be trapped in a season and not progress unless you have a breakthrough—a breaking out of whatever has trapped you in that season. You may need a breakthrough out of fear and into faith.

Sixteen-year-old Shawn Johnson won two silver medals in gymnastics at the Beijing Olympics in 2008. In her second promotional video clip aired before the Olympic Games, speaking about how she succeeded when others failed, Johnson said,

> Gymnastics is about falling. Sometimes it's scary, at times it's embarrassing, and it hurts. But you have to do it over and over again. If you are afraid to fall, you'll never get better. Why am I going to the Olympics? Because I'm not afraid to fall.

The Breaker Anointing Is upon You
to Break Off Spiritual Layers of Bondage That Hinder You

We find our breakthroughs by accepting Christ's work on the cross for us and then walking in Christ to maintain our freedom.

Breakthroughs are needed in our lives because we are born as sinners, and sin is the primary cause of spiritual bondage. We find our breakthroughs by accepting Christ's work on the cross for us and then walking in Christ to maintain our freedom. There can be times when born-again believers find themselves in stages of bondage. The person who gives in to sinful activity and habits will become bound with those sinful bondages. Jesus spoke of this in the gospel of John. (See also Isaiah 58:6–8; Jeremiah 34:13.)

> *Jesus said to those Jews who believed Him, "If you abide in My word, you are My disciples indeed. And you shall know the truth, and the truth shall make you free....Therefore if the Son makes you free, you shall be free indeed."* (John 8:31–32, 36)

Spiritual freedom is achieved as the believer breaks through and overcomes the evil spiritual capacity within, which is called *the flesh.*

The flesh is the tendency within each person to operate independently of God and center his or her interest on the self. When you were born again, your old self died and your new self came to life, but during the time you spent separated from God, your worldly experiences programmed you with thought patterns, responses, and habits that are alien to God. Therefore, even though the old lord of your life is gone, your flesh remains in opposition to God in a preprogrammed propensity to sin. (See Romans 8:3, 6:6; Ephesians 4:22; Romans 7:17.)

We are to give no *"place to the devil"* (Ephesians 4:27), because he will use any ground we give him. Willfully giving way to practice sins of the flesh gives occasion for Satan to have his way in a believer's life. Although Satan's entire legal claim against us was cancelled at the cross, believers' willful indulgence in fleshly sins gives the enemy a place or a claim against us that he will be quick to exploit.

Your breakthrough is by the power of Christ and the authority of the Breaker anointing upon you. Decide to separate from sinful influences. Decide to cleanse yourself from all defilement of the flesh. Decide to rededicate your life to serve God and God alone. Break out of the past. (See 2 Corinthians 6:17, 7:1; Romans 12:1; Hebrews 12:1.)

The Breaker Anointing Is upon You to Break Through to New Open Doors

Class had been over for fifteen minutes, but the young college student hung around, talking in the hallway. Suddenly, realizing the time, she ran down the hall toward the parking lot, desperate to make up for lost time so she wouldn't be late to work. As she hurried through the open doorway, she slammed against an invisible force that stopped her in her tracks. Dazed from the blow, she stood in front of the doorway, staring at it. Why couldn't she go through it? Tentatively, she put out her hand, not sure what to expect. Then, her hand touched...glass. This was not an open door. It was a full-length window. The door was to her right.

How many times have you tried to go through a door that wasn't a door? Or have you ever grasped a doorknob to push the door open, only to slam into the locked door? What is your first reaction when that happens? If you're like me, it's to look around and see if anyone noticed what you just did!

There are spiritual doors that God wants to open up in this season of your life. Some will open easily. Others will be more difficult to open, but they are still doors that God has set before you. Many doors will open and close in your lifetime. Some need to be opened, and others need to be shut. Some you need to go through, and others you need to avoid. By the guidance of the Holy Spirit, you can know which doors to move through, which doors to lock, which doors to push open, and which doors to leave alone.

This is a time for opening new doors—doors in our lives, our families, our businesses, or our churches. The church should always be ready for new doors to open. We are embarking on a journey into new areas where we have never been before and praying about opportunities that we have never had before. What about you as an individual? What door does the Lord have for your life during this season? What opportunities could be in front of you, waiting for you to knock, waiting for you to enter?

> *God will set before you an open door, but you must determine to walk through it.*

Say yes to the new doors that God desires to open for you, now and in the future. He will set before you an open door, but you must determine to walk through it. You must choose to respond as the psalmist did in Psalm 24:7: "*Lift up your heads, O you gates! And be lifted up, you everlasting doors! And the King of glory shall come in.*"

The New Doors Set Before You

I know your works. See, I have set before you an open door, and no one can shut it; for you have a little strength, have kept My word, and have not denied My name. (Revelation 3:8)

"*I have set before you.*" Write these words on your heart and meditate on them. *God has set before me an open door that no one can shut.* All of us are precious in the sight of the Lord—every single one of us. God has a plan and a strategy for your life. Before the foundation of the world, our lives were laid out in eternity. God knows you. He knows the year that lies ahead of you. He knows your month, your day, and your hour, and He's involved in every minute of your life. God fills every second, and He has set a door before you. Your prayer should be, "Lord, show me the door You have set before me."

"For a great and effective door has opened to me, and there are many adversaries" (1 Corinthians 16:9). This verse was written during a pivotal time in the apostle Paul's life. He was in Ephesus, teaching the young church growing in that city and seeing phenomenal results. In Acts 19:11, Scripture says that *"unusual miracles"* were taking place. Also,

> *Many of those who had practiced magic brought their books together and burned them in the sight of all. And they counted up the value of them, and it totaled fifty thousand pieces of silver. So the word of the Lord grew mightily and prevailed.*
> (Acts 19:19–20)

Indeed, these were *"great and effective"* doors! Many miracles happened, the Word of the Lord grew mightily, many believed, and lives were changed.

However, there is a second part to 1 Corinthians 16:9: *"there are many adversaries."* It was in Ephesus that Demetrius the silversmith stirred up a riot against Paul, creating such havoc that the whole city was filled with confusion.

A great door and many adversaries. If the door is great, the adversaries are many. Little door, little adversaries. Great door, great adversaries. For every effective door that God has planned for you, there are opponents and adversaries who desire to shut the door and stop you from entering.

> *If the door is great, the adversaries are many.*

What Are Your New Doors?

"See, I have set before you an open door" (Revelation 3:8). Whoever you are, God has set an open door before you. It doesn't matter

whether you are a teenager, a young adult, a young married person, or a widow; employed, unemployed, prospering in business, or bankrupt; happy or unhappy, satisfied or dissatisfied, filled with expectation, or having an empty soul.

Whoever you are, wherever you are, God has set an open door before you. God is saying, "I have set a door before you, and I will keep it open for you. Even when you are discouraged, even when you don't have the strength to muster up the ability to put one foot in front of another, I'll keep it open by grace until you're able to enter into it."

Sometimes, an open door is set before you, but you are so troubled or weak that you can hardly walk through it. You might cry out, "Oh, God, why didn't You open this door six months ago? I could have walked through it then. I would have had the strength then." But God says, "I will hold the door open for you." Sometimes, we look in despair at closed doors and say, "I knocked on the wrong door too many times. What if this isn't the right door? What if I missed the right door because I was knocking on the wrong door?"

Maybe you knocked a few times on the wrong door, or maybe you didn't go through at the right time, but God doesn't slam the door on you. He loves you too much. He wants you to find the doors that He has for your life. As you stand on the threshold of a new season in your life, what doors could God have in front of you? What relational doors are before you? What business doors or spiritual doors?

A Door of New Faith Adventures

Now when they had come and gathered the church together, they reported all that God had done with them, and that He had opened the door of faith to the Gentiles. (Acts 14:27)

God opened a door of faith in an arena that had never been opened before. No one had ever tried to go through that door. Peter was the first to go to the Gentiles, and the response was overwhelming. Prior to that time, the gospel had been taken only to the Jews. But Peter stepped through the door of faith to preach the message of the gospel to the Gentiles.

What faith doors does God want to open in your life? In order to step through a faith door, you have to step out of your comfort zone. It is easy to say, "Oh God, give me faith, but don't make me change. Oh Lord, let me have faith to walk on water, but don't make me get out of the boat."

We want to have faith, but we don't want to take the road that gets us there. To step into the realm of faith, we have to step out of our comfort zones. Where is your comfort zone? It is the area where you feel most comfortable trusting God. There are areas where you feel comfortable moving out in faith, yet there are other areas that make us very nervous.

Your comfort zone might be sitting in your pew. You always sit in the same seat around the same people. It's safe. It's comfortable. Or, your comfort zone might be praying only with people at church, never at work. It's not comfortable to ask an unsaved coworker, "I'm sorry your father has cancer; can I pray for him?" It's not comfortable, but how can we see miracles happen if we don't take risks?

Move out of your comfort zone. Take a leap of faith. Leap into the new. Open a door and move through it. Take a risk and move into the unknown. The African impala, a type of antelope, can jump more than eight feet high, yet it can be kept in a pen with walls that are only three feet high. Why? Impalas are afraid to jump if they cannot see where they will land. They cannot take the risk of jumping unless they know exactly where their feet will fall.

A quotation attributed to Hudson Taylor, founder of the China Inland Mission, says it best: "Unless there is an element of risk in our exploits for God, there is no need for faith." The results of Taylor stepping into the unknown and moving out of his comfort zone are amazing. When he died, China Inland Mission had grown from only one man to 205 missionary stations, 849 missionaries, and 125,000 Chinese Christians.

> *Unless there is an element of risk in our exploits for God, there is no need for faith.*

The greatest faith adventures require a step into the unknown, a step of faith—yet imagine the results! What could God do through your life if you took the risk of walking through the new door He has set before you?

A Door of Great Opportunities

What might keep me back from great opportunities? Good opportunities. There is an old adage that says, "Good is the greatest enemy of great." We have thousands of schools in America that are good; we don't have thousands that are great. We have thousands of hamburger businesses or pizza businesses or computer businesses, but only a few become great. Many people have good marriages, but do they have great ones? Many people have good prayer lives, but not great ones. What is the greatest enemy of great? Good.

The enemy of great opportunities is learning to love the good—to the extent that it satisfies your soul and there is no desire to go through another door. *Good* becomes satisfied with a certain level and never moves past it. Ask yourself, *Have I changed in my prayer life, worship life, evangelism life, or service life in the past five years, or am I about the same? Do I have more intensity in worship, more penetration in evangelism, or a greater giving of myself? Am I growing, or have I settled for a status quo life?* Few people attain greatness because it is too easy to have a good life. Don't settle for *good*. Don't settle for *easy*.

> *Few people attain greatness because it is too easy to have a good life. Don't settle for good.*

A Door of New Hope

I will give her her vineyards from there, and the Valley of Achor as a door of hope; she shall sing there, as in the days of her youth, as in the day when she came up from the land of Egypt.
(Hosea 2:15)

Achor was not just a place of sorrow; it was a place of devastation and grief. It was the place where Achan and his family were stoned to death after his sin was discovered. Yet there, in the place of devastation and death, God opened a door of hope. In our "Achors," in the deepest, darkest, meanest, and cruelest valleys, where there is nothing but tears and grief, we can miss the doors that are set before us—doors of hope and opportunity.

We ask how God can allow devastation to happen to us. *Why did this sorrowful thing happen? Why did this crisis arise? Why did this disappointment, this trial, overtake me? Why do I have to walk through this dark valley that overwhelms me?* As you stand in your Valley of Achor, remember that verse from Hosea. When you find yourself in the deepest, darkest, meanest, and cruelest valley, where there seems to be no hope and no door, when you find yourself standing alone in the midst of grief, remember that there will be a door of hope at the bottom of the valley. When no one else can show you the way out, when you don't know how you are going to survive, remember that there is a special door made just for that valley. It's a door of hope.

Your Valley of Achor might be a place of failure, but even there, God opens a door of hope. In the midst of your failure can be the grace for your greatest success. In your failures can be the seeds of the greatest mission of your life.

Chuck Colson seemed to be at the pinnacle of a great life. As an aide to President Nixon, he was seen as one of the most powerful and feared men in the nation during his four years of service in the White House. Then, in 1974, he was imprisoned for Watergate-related charges. In his own book, he said,

> The real legacy of my life was my biggest failure—that I was an ex-convict. My greatest humiliation—being sent to prison—was the beginning of God's greatest use of my life; He chose the one experience in which I could not glory for His glory.[19]

It was his darkest hour. The day he was sentenced to prison was a day of hopelessness and humiliation. It meant the death of dreams for a man considered to be one of the greatest thinkers of the twentieth century. This great man, this awesome politician, had gone off track, had made a horrible mistake, and was being thrown into prison. His life was destroyed. His hopes, dreams, and ambitions were gone.

While he was in prison, however, the seeds of his true greatness were sown. He now has the greatest ministry to prisoners in the world. He has written books in the last few years that have affected the mind-set of the body of Christ. He has spoken truth when people didn't want to hear it. And he says that his darkest hour was his door of hope—and he didn't even know it.

What disappointment, hurt, or deep, dark valley has taken over your life and caused you to give up? Out of that heap of ashes can come a new mission, a new mercy, and a new hope.

A Door of the Lord's Choosing

I came to Troas to preach Christ's gospel, and a door was opened to me by the Lord. (2 Corinthians 2:12)

> *A door of the Lord's choosing is simply a door He chooses for you.*

A door of the Lord's choosing is simply a door He chooses for you. It is not a door that you chose for yourself. You didn't knock on that door. You didn't turn the handle. You weren't on a path toward that door. In fact, you didn't even know that door existed. And if you had known it existed, you would not have chosen it, because it is not the door of your choice; it's the door of His choice.

Perhaps a job you lost has become the seed in the ground to start the business you never would have started otherwise. The door could be the abuse you went through in the past, which is now the seed for starting you toward one of the greatest ministries of counseling, healing, and helping that you could ever have imagined in your life. Out of the hurt comes a surprise door—a door of His choosing.

It could be a surprise door, one you never would have imagined. I have been surprised. Becoming the senior pastor of City Bible Church was a surprise door in my life. When we moved to Eugene, Oregon, my wife, Sharon, and I never planned on coming to Portland. We pioneered a church there, lived there for twelve years, and had our children there. It was home for us. We never thought about another door. We didn't want another door, but all of a sudden, God opened up a surprise door.

Chuck Colson never thought that God would open up a surprise door through the season of his greatest failure. Yet as a result, he founded Prison Fellowship Ministries, the world's largest outreach to prisoners and their families, with ministries in ninety-three countries. Additionally, he has written sixteen books.

What doors might the Lord open for you this year? What doors of His choosing are around the next corner?

Personal Testimony

Travis,
Twenty-Five Years Old

A year after high school, I decided to spend the next season of life at Portland Bible College. My desire was to enroll as a music major because I was certain that God would use me mightily as an influential worship leader and songwriter. I don't know why I was so certain—He had never told me that! But I had been involved in leading worship up until that point, and since it was something I enjoyed, I simply assumed that it had to be a major piece of my destiny.

I can remember the process of enrolling for courses as an incoming freshman. I was sitting in line, waiting for my turn to see the next available faculty adviser so he could approve the classes I was requesting; but my registration form was still blank. Every other student had the form filled out with the classes he or she would be taking, but I just couldn't decide which courses to write down.

As I was sitting there, thoughts began to pour into my mind of recent opportunities I had been given to teach or preach at youth meetings or to my small group. I wasn't entirely sure, but as I waited in line, I began to perceive that the reason God wanted me to attend school was to develop a gift of teaching. I flipped to the section in my registration packet that displayed the theology courses and barely had my form filled out before the faculty adviser called, "Next." It was settled. I was a theology major.

I distinctly recall the excitement I felt as a freshman attending the theology courses. I was learning so much, and even the stuff I already knew was taking on a new dimension of meaning in my mind. My knowledge and understanding were growing, but something else was growing inside of me. That thought I had encountered while waiting in line at registration was morphing into something beyond the thought realm. It was transforming into faith. I could study like my teachers had studied. I could teach like my teachers were teaching. The Spirit of God could use me to open minds, break off strongholds, declare truth, and inspire faith.

As my years at Portland Bible College passed, the awareness of my calling grew—though the details of how God might work it out remained mysterious. I couldn't pull any strings to find an expression for my gift; if that was an option, I wasn't aware of it. So, I just gave myself to serving the church wherever it was needed. One day, during my junior year, I was praying when the Lord surprised me with a question: "What do you want?"

I thought for a moment. Then, when I had the right response, I answered, "I would like wisdom, Lord."

He quickly replied, "That was Solomon's answer. I asked you what *you* wanted."

He knew what I wanted. But He was teaching me a lesson. I began to tell Him in detail how I wanted my life to play out in regard to calling, ministry, and vocation. I knew I hadn't exactly been given heaven's blank check, but I felt like God was actually listening to me, more than eager to fulfill these desires. After all, they were desires that *He* had been forming within me. Out of all the things I asked for, the most significant in my mind was this: I wanted to teach full-time at Portland Bible College. After I admitted this to God, He simply conveyed the thought, "Okay, done."

I had spent years in Bible college focusing on God—His nature, His attributes, His overarching purpose and plan. Yet what one believes about God is only a fraction of his faith. Hebrews 11:6 states that *"without faith it is impossible to please Him, for he who comes to God must believe that He is, **and that He is a rewarder of those who diligently seek Him***" (emphasis added). God was stretching my faith to believe that He actually wanted to be my Rewarder and to make my dreams a reality.

To make a long story short, the months after my graduation were full of incredible opportunities. Doors were flying open before me, and I somehow ended up working as an assistant to the senior pastor at my church. After a year, a teaching position opened up at Portland Bible College. With my head spinning and not being exactly sure what had happened, I found myself in that position.

I can't help but wonder how things might have been different if I had ignored the thought I received from the Lord as I registered for classes, or where I might be now without a firm faith in God as my Rewarder.

Keys to Opening New Doors

One thing I do, forgetting those things which are behind and reaching forward to those things which are ahead, I press toward the goal for the prize of the upward call of God in Christ Jesus.
(Philippians 3:13–14)

You can't enter a new door until you've shut the old one. You can't go through the new door when you are standing with your back to it and facing the old door. Shut the

You can't enter a new door until you've shut the old one.

doors of destructive relationships. Reconcile past offenses. Close the door of unforgiveness, bitterness, and resentment, and move ahead into a new future.

Shut the doors of bad habits and old patterns or ways of doing things. Close the door of wrong ways of thinking and acting, and begin to make new habits and new patterns of thinking. Shut the door of regret. Yesterday's mistakes don't need to control today. Yesterday's hurts need to be left there. Stop griping about the way things are. Quit complaining about what could have been. Instead, look at the grace of God and remember that it is by His grace that you are who you are, and it is by His grace that He will use you just the way you are.

The Believer's Keys: Ask, Seek, Knock

Matthew 7:7 is the simplest Scripture I know to put the key into your hands: *"Ask, and it will be given to you; seek, and you will find; knock, and it will be opened to you."* The Amplified Bible reads, *"Keep on asking and it will be given you; keep on seeking and you will find; keep on knocking [reverently] and [the door] will be opened to you."*

What specific thing are you asking the Lord? For a year, I have been carrying a sheet of paper in my Bible. One year ago, a young woman in our church approached me and said, "Pastor Frank, this morning, you told the singles to pray specifically for husbands. Here are the qualities I want. Will you pray with me?" She had written out a great list, and she began praying it. She is now married with two children.

Ask confidently. Make your plans large. Pray big prayers. Hudson Taylor said,

> The prayer power has never been tried to its full capacity. If we want to see mighty wonders of the divine power and grace wrought in the places of weakness, failure and disappointment, let us answer God's standing challenge, *"Call unto me, and I will answer thee, and show thee great and mighty things, which thou knowest not"* (Jeremiah 33:3 KJV).[20]

In Joshua 17, the tribes of Ephraim and Manasseh approached Joshua as the land was being divided into portions for each tribe, asking, *"Why have you given us only one lot and one share to inherit, since we are a great people, inasmuch as the LORD has blessed us until now?"* (verse 14). Joshua responded, *"You are a great people and have great power; you shall not have only one lot, but the mountain country shall be yours"* (verses 17–18). One lot wasn't enough! God has blessed us. He is going to continue to bless us. The people from Ephraim and Manasseh asked greatly, and God gave greatly.

A. B. Simpson, global evangelist and founder of the Christian and Missionary Alliance, once said,

> Do we know the power of our supernatural weapon? Do we dare to use it with the authority of a faith that commands as well as asks? God grant us holy audacity and divine confidence. He is not wanting great men, but He is wanting people who will dare to prove the greatness of their God.

How great is your God? Have you asked according to His greatness or according to your own comfort level? What are you asking? Are you asking small or large? C. S. Lewis wrote,

Are you asking according to God's greatness or according to your own comfort level?

> Indeed if we consider the unblushing promises of reward and the staggering nature of the rewards promised in the Gospels, it would seem that Our Lord finds our desires not too strong, but too weak. We are half-hearted creatures, fooling about with drink and sex and ambition when infinite joy is offered us, like an ignorant child who wants to go on making mud pies in a slum because he cannot imagine what is meant by the offer of a holiday at the sea. We are far too easily pleased.[21]

Are you settling for mud pies, or are you ready to head for a holiday by the sea? Are you asking large? Are you asking according to the promises of Jesus Himself?

Most assuredly, I say to you, he who believes in Me, the works that I do he will do also; and greater works than these he will do, because I go to My Father. And whatever you ask in My name, that I will do, that the Father may be glorified in the Son. If you ask anything in My name, I will do it. (John 14:12–14)

What are you asking for? What are you seeking? Are you knocking on doors? If you could have anything you ask for, what would you request? What door would you knock on? In Matthew 7:7, God Himself promised, "Ask, because I'm waiting to hear you ask so I can give. Seek, so I can be found by you. Knock, and I have some great doors to open for you."

New Door Adversaries

In *The Pilgrim's Progress* by John Bunyan, Christian approached a house and began to knock at the gates. As he did, an interesting thing happened. Dogs began to bark. And the more he knocked, the more the dogs barked. The louder he knocked, the louder the dogs barked. Sometimes, we knock on doors, and our adversary intimidates us into stopping. He causes a commotion, and things begin to happen that we don't expect.

In *The Message* Bible, 1 Corinthians 16:9 reads, *"A huge door of opportunity for good work has opened up here. There is also mushrooming opposition."* An adversary is an opponent. He is someone who strives against you, attempting to bind and limit you. He wants to put you into a tight place and shut you in. In wrestling, the goal of your opponent is to get you pinned down on the ground so you can't move—so you are trapped with nowhere to go and no way to escape. Your adversary attempts to do the same thing. He wants to limit your opportunities, bind your potential, and pin you into a tight place where you have no way out.

If you are filled with faith to knock on new doors, you must be filled with the strength to fight. If you start knocking on the very fruitful door called "the will of God for your life," resistance will come. When you knock on great doors, there will be great resistance. The greater the door, the greater the resistance. The more at stake, the more the enemy will come and try to prevent you from entering that door.

Following are some adversaries that will lurk at the best doors of your life. Recognize them so that when you see them coming, you will overcome them, for the doors that the Lord has for you are awesome doors.

The Adversary of Unconquered Fear

Do you realize that the most frequently repeated instruction in the Bible is the command to *"fear not"*? Why is that so? It is because we are all prone to fear. We fear failure, the future, and the unknown. We fear fear itself. The number one reason people refuse to go through new doors is that they are afraid. They are afraid to make changes; they're afraid to step out of the boat.

The Adversary of Spiritual Stagnation

Is your life one of unrealized potential? Of unfulfilled longings? Do you have a sense that you are not living your life as you were supposed to live it—that there is far more you could be living? Spiritual stagnation is caused by sinful patterns of behavior that are never confronted or changed. Stagnation never cultivates or deploys your abilities and gifts. Spiritual stagnation is the great, bold prayers that you never prayed, the exhilarating risks you never took, the sacrificial gifts you never offered, the lives you never touched, and the dreams you left lying on your pillow at night and never brought into the light of day.

> *Spiritual stagnation is the great, bold prayers that you never prayed, the lives you never touched, and the dreams you left lying on your pillow at night.*

The fear of stepping through the new door waits for a guarantee of not failing. So, you wait for the perfect opportunity, the perfect door...and you wait and you wait, because there is always an element of risk. Soon, you forget what you are waiting for, and you simply wait, stagnating, losing vitality, losing life until you would not recognize the new door if it had a fluorescent sign on it that read, "This is your new door!" And if you did recognize it, it would cost you too much to walk through it.

There is a story of an ancient Persian named Al Hafed who heard about diamonds—their great value and their great beauty. So, he went to a priest in his village and asked him, "Where can I find diamonds?" The priest replied, "Find a river that runs over white sand between high mountains; in those sands, you will always see diamonds." Al Hafed sold his farm, left his family, and began to search for the right river—the one that ran over white sand and came from high mountains. He searched for his entire life. He searched in country after country until he died a destitute and broken man.

Back at his home in Persia, the man who had bought Al Hafed's farm took his camels out to the garden to water them. As the first camel's nose disturbed the water, the man caught a glimpse of something shiny in the streambed. Reaching into the river, he pulled out a strange stone that reflected light in beautiful colors. He took it home and put it on a shelf, where it caught the eye of a guest in his home. Recognizing the value of the stone, the guest rushed the farmer out to the garden, where they dug through the dirt and found diamond after diamond.

According to legend, thus were the diamond mines of Golconda found—on Al Hafed's farm. The river that went over white sands as it flowed from the high mountains had been in front of him all his life, but he did not recognize it. He died a man without hope—a man who had given up because he never recognized the door that was in front of his eyes every day.

The Adversary of Small Dreams

Ask God to give you God-size dreams, not dreams that fit you.

Small dreams can be fulfilled with small faith and small sacrifice from small efforts by small people with small futures. Get rid of the smallness of your spirit and reach ahead. Ask God to give you God-size dreams, not dreams that fit you. If your dream is so small that you can fulfill it yourself, it is too small. A God-size dream cannot be accomplished without God. An old prayer attributed to Sir Francis Drake goes as follows:

Disturb us, Lord, when we are too well pleased with ourselves, when our dreams have come true because we have dreamed too little, when we arrive safely because we have sailed too closely to the shore.

Disturb us, Lord, when with the abundance of things we posses we have lost our thirst for life; having fallen in love with life, we have ceased to dream of eternity; and in our efforts to build a new earth, we have allowed our vision of the new heaven to dim.

Disturb us, Lord, to dare more boldly, to venture on wider and deeper seas where storms will show your mastery; where losing sight of land we shall find the stars. We ask you to push back the horizons of our hopes; and to push into the future and strength, courage, hope, and love.

The Adversary of "It's Too Late for Me"

Never allow your past to govern your future. Read the Bible. It is full of people whose pasts were bad but who still were used greatly by God. Two of the women who are found in the lineage of Jesus are Rahab and Bathsheba. Who were they? Rahab was a harlot, and Bathsheba was an adulteress; yet look what God brought about through them! God has an amazing way of using anyone who has a heart for Him.

Never think that you are too old for a new door. At age sixty-nine, Ronald Reagan was elected president of the United States. He was reelected when he was seventy-three. Grandma Moses did not begin to paint until the age of seventy-seven, yet she became a world famous painter, producing more than one thousand works before she died at age 101. At age ninety-nine, Harold Foster of Owensboro, Kentucky, began to learn to read, and at age 102, Alice Porlock of Great Britain published her first book.

What dreams have you nurtured deep inside, hoping against hope that one day they might become reality? What doors have you gazed at longingly, wishing you were younger so you could walk through them? Don't let age stop you!

After she was widowed at age seventy-seven, Margaret Cole went to Papua New Guinea with Wycliffe Bible Translators to assist with bookkeeping for several years. She then went to the Mam Indians in Guatemala to help a nurse run a clinic. She retired again but later went to teach English to Cambodian refugees in a rustic camp on the border of Thailand. At eighty, she delivered eight Bibles to Burma (now Myanmar).

God can open any door. And if He opens it, He will give you the grace and strength to walk through it.

The Adversary of an Empty Soul

An empty soul does not have the life or virtue even to begin hoping for a door, much less the impetus to walk through a door if one was available. If you are living on past victories or past failures, your soul is probably empty. If you have let your Bible reading and your prayer life drop off, your soul is probably on its way to empty. If you allow little things—little trials, little irritations—to discourage you, your soul gauge is reading empty.

The empty soul is the devil's work, and he will use it when a door of opportunity opens. Fill your soul today with new virtue and new strength. Open your Bible and begin feeding your spirit, renewing your mind, and strengthening your faith.

The Adversary of Settling for Good Instead of Pushing for Great

Good is satisfying. It is easy, and you can live it right now without having to change. *Great* means that you will have to confront some current realities about yourself and change. Perhaps your current reality is your small dreams, your empty soul, or your fear. The only way to move ahead is to confront your current reality, looking into the mirror of the Word of God, and ask God to help you change. Through faith, confession, and the power of the Holy Spirit, you can change.

Position yourself to move through a new door. Commit to moving through any door that God opens for you. Refuse to allow your adversaries to stop you.

I challenge you to rise to a new level of faith and courage. I challenge you to face your adversaries head-on and remove them from your door. I challenge you to open the door set before you and move through it by faith.

Chapter 7

Yes to Surplus Living

Surplus living is a biblical concept taught by Christ and the apostles. *Surplus* is a kingdom principle that all believers should endeavor to see become reality in their lives. Jesus said,

The thief does not come except to steal, and to kill, and to destroy. I have come that they may have life, and that they may have it more abundantly. (John 10:10)

Life abundant and life *more* abundant is God's will for you. You are called to be a person of surplus in every aspect of living; you are to have a surplus soul, a surplus of joy, a surplus of prayer, a surplus of resources, a surplus of strength, and a surplus of encouragement.

Surplus is more than is required or needed—over and above the norm. Surplus spills over the top. It is more than sufficient. It is excessive, beyond what you have expected.

A surplus person believes Ephesians 3:20, which says, *"Now to Him who is able to do exceedingly abundantly above all that we ask or think, according to the power that works in us."* Believe that God is a great God and a good God. He is a God of abundance and an all-things-are-possible God. Believe that God desires to bless you and increase your capacity to full and overflowing surplus.

> *Believe for surplus so you can be a blessing to other people in need. You cannot give what you do not have.*

Why should you believe for surplus? So that you can be a blessing to other people in

133

need. You cannot give what you do not have. If you live empty, always in a place of lack and scarcity, how will you bless others?

Don't Think the Way the World Thinks

We are conditioned to think in terms of lack and limitation because we live in a worldly system that influences our thinking in this way. We see lack in everything around us. Everything is running out of surplus. We continually hear the words *lack, scarcity, running out, extinct, used up, shortage,* and *not enough.* We hear them until we begin to believe them. We are conditioned by the continual message that the world feeds us—the message of lack—so we hold on to everything we have for fear that it will run out.

Cell phones have limited minutes and limited calling areas. Cars have limited gas supplies. Insurance has limited coverage. Our oil supply is limited. Our water supply is limited. Our clean air is limited. Everything around us is limited, scarce, and running out. So, instead of developing mind-sets of surplus, we live with mind-sets of lack that make us cling to what we have.

This lack and scarcity thinking produces lack and scarcity people. You have a choice. You can let the world's system of thought influence your thinking and ultimately your living, or you can break out into the new world of God's thoughts, God's ways, and God's abilities. The apostle Paul challenged us not to give in to the world's system:

> *I beseech you therefore, brethren, by the mercies of God, that you present your bodies a living sacrifice, holy, acceptable to God, which is your reasonable service. And do not be conformed to this world, but be transformed by the renewing of your mind, that you may prove what is that good and acceptable and perfect will of God.*   (Romans 12:1–2)

You can choose right this minute to live according to God's laws of surplus and not according to the world's laws of lack. You choose. Pray the following prayer as a first step toward becoming a person of surplus.

Father God, I desire to live the life that You have planned for me—a life that is overflowing and abundant. Break me out of the lack mentality and teach me how to live with surplus. Show me how to live life to the fullest with ample resources for my journey and surplus resources to bless and help others, because I cannot give what I do not have. Amen.

We must be transformed by the renewing of our minds to see the kingdom of God operate on the principle of plentiful supply—the principle of surplus.

You crown the year with Your goodness, and Your paths drip with abundance. (Psalm 65:11)

Then you shall see and become radiant, and your heart shall swell with joy; because the abundance of the sea shall be turned to you, the wealth of the Gentiles shall come to you. (Isaiah 60:5)

...a land in which you will eat bread without scarcity, in which you will lack nothing; a land whose stones are iron and out of whose hills you can dig copper. (Deuteronomy 8:9)

When you go, you will come to a secure people and a large land. For God has given it into your hands, a place where there is no lack of anything that is on the earth. (Judges 18:10)

As it is written, "He who gathered much had nothing left over, and he who gathered little had no lack." (2 Corinthians 8:15)

For thus says the LORD God of Israel: "The bin of flour shall not be used up, nor shall the jar of oil run dry, until the day the LORD sends rain on the earth." (1 Kings 17:14)

And my God shall supply all your need according to His riches in glory by Christ Jesus. (Philippians 4:19)

Commit your way to the LORD, trust also in Him, and He shall bring it to pass. (Psalm 37:5)

Become a Surplus Person

In the mid-1800s, the Great Potato Famine devastated Ireland. One out of every four people fled the country to avoid dying of starvation. Of those who stayed, many were evicted from their farms because they could not pay the rent for their small parcels of land. Fear of financial loss caused many landowners to evict any farmers who could not make their rent payments because of the crop failures.

However, one landowner refused to accept the spirit of scarcity that had captured his fellow landowners. John Bloomfield, the owner of Castle Caldwell in County Fermanagh, realized the desperate situation of his tenants and was looking for ideas to help them survive. As an amateur mineralogist, he noticed that the exteriors of his tenant farmers' small cottages had vivid, white finishes, and he had a geological survey done.

Upon learning of the rich mineral deposits in the land, he built a pottery in the village of Belleek to provide employment for his tenants. The porcelain china they produced has been described as translucent with an iridescent finish, and its delicate strength produces extravagant designs. The high quality porcelain drew customers from as far away as Australia and included the British royal family. This multimillion-dollar industry arose from a man who believed for surplus in a time of lack so that he could be a blessing to others.

We are called to a higher mark for an eternal purpose.

The world tells you to receive and keep everything you can. The world tells you to look out for number one, because no one else will look out for you. It tells you to get ahead in life by any means you can and then protect everything you have before it runs out. This is not how a surplus person thinks or lives. We are called to a higher mark for an eternal purpose.

I see four different kinds of people every day. Which kind are you? Are you a **minus person**, who is always lacking emotionally, spiritually, financially, and relationally? Do you never have enough? Or, are you a **plus person**, who has just enough to be healthy, happy, and secure? Do you have just a little extra to give selectively when and to whom you choose? Or, are you a **surplus person**, who lives life to the fullest with more than enough for yourself and for those around you? Are you joyful and energized, serving others and extending the kingdom of God? Or, finally, are you a **super-surplus person**, who has an excessive overflow that runs over the top? Do you freely and liberally bless others around you and those around the world? Do you have a flow that never stops gushing forth?

I am sure that, without hesitation, you would choose to be the surplus or super-surplus person. Make a commitment to identify the minus issues in your spirit and soul, and then, by prayer and obedience to the Word of God, remove those minuses. Move from minus living to plus living, and then from plus living to surplus living, and then move on to super-surplus living. Believe the Scriptures that God has given to you and shoot for the mark that God's Word has set for your life.

There is one who scatters, yet increases more; and there is one who withholds more than is right, but it leads to poverty. The generous soul will be made rich, and he who waters will also be watered himself. (Proverbs 11:24–25)

Give, and it will be given to you: good measure, pressed down, shaken together, and running over will be put into your bosom. For with the same measure that you use, it will be measured back to you. (Luke 6:38)

The blessing of the Lord *makes one rich, and He adds no sorrow with it.* (Proverbs 10:22)

For the Lord *God is a sun and shield; the* Lord *will give grace and glory; no good thing will He withhold from those who walk uprightly.* (Psalm 84:11)

Honor the Lord *with your possessions, and with the firstfruits of all your increase; so your barns will be filled with plenty, and your vats will overflow with new wine.* (Proverbs 3:9–10)

He who sows sparingly will also reap sparingly, and he who sows bountifully will also reap bountifully. (2 Corinthians 9:6)

All these blessings shall come upon you and overtake you, because you obey the voice of the LORD your God.
(Deuteronomy 28:2)

I will give you the treasures of darkness and hidden riches of secret places, that you may know that I, the LORD, who call you by your name, am the God of Israel. (Isaiah 45:3)

The soul of a surplus person is described in Psalm 45:1: *"My heart is overflowing with a good theme."* In *The Message* Bible, this verse reads, *"My heart bursts its banks, spilling beauty and goodness."*

The Surplus Soul

God wants your life to have an overflowing, surplus theme. In 3 John 2, the apostle John prayed, *"Beloved, I pray that you may prosper in all things and be in health, just as your soul prospers."* The surplus soul is the source of the surplus life. The surplus soul must be healthy and overflowing.

This begins with a right relationship with God through Jesus. Jesus said, *"Behold, I stand at the door and knock. If anyone hears My voice and opens the door, I will come in to him and dine with him, and he with Me"* (Revelation 3:20). When we are born again, our spirits are joined to the Holy Spirit as new creations that are alive and thirsting after spiritual things, such as knowing God and loving God.

God has redeemed you so that you may become a person with a surplus soul who lives a surplus life. Spiritually, emotionally, financially, and relationally, you can have a life that is full, abundant, and overflowing. God loves you just the way you are, but He will not leave you that way. He wants to change whatever hinders your surplus life. God's love never ceases. Never! Although you may spurn Him, ignore Him, reject Him, despise Him, or disobey Him, He still loves you because He is God.

God loves you! If you have never accepted Christ, or if you are away from Christ, pray the following prayer right now.

Father, I bring You my life. I ask that You would come into my heart and cleanse me from all my sin through the blood of Christ. I leave the past behind me. I shut the door to my past and open a new door to my future with You as my Lord and Savior. Amen.

A surplus life begins with knowing the God of surplus and then tapping into His infinite supply of all that we need for our lives and for others.

Don't be like the wealthy but frugal woman who lived in a small house on the seashore in Ireland at the turn of the century. She was talked into putting electricity into her house, and after several weeks, the meter man came to read her meter. Puzzled, he knocked on the door and asked her how the electricity was working. She responded, "It's working perfectly. Why?" He replied, "Your meter shows that you are scarcely using any power. Are you using your electric lights?" "Certainly!" she answered emphatically. "Every sunset, I turn my lights on just long enough to light my candles, and then I turn the lights off to save the power."

She had unlimited power, but she was not benefiting from that power. Her house was connected, but the power was not being utilized. It's not enough to just *know* the God of surplus. Tap into the power that He has given you!

Personal Testimony

Scott,
Young Businessman in His Thirties

I'm a third-generation surplus thinker, so it's practically embedded in my DNA. My wife and I have grown up with an understanding that this is just how you "do life."

I remember cleaning out my grandparents' house after my grandpa was hospitalized for a short time. As we searched through paperwork to make sure nothing of importance was discarded, I found receipts going back almost forty years. Every third one was for helping underprivileged children, evangelistic ministries, or local church donations with support that would challenge even the biggest of givers! Thousands of dollars a month were given from a steel worker's paycheck and the revenue from a small farm in North Dakota. Moreover, my grandma's full-time job was being a volunteer at Loaves and Fishes and at any other ministry at the church where she could be of help.

My parents have also been surplus thinkers, and I suppose most of my faith for surplus has come by watching them. They have done so much in their lives that it is hard to believe that they could simultaneously be surplus parents. They were parents to over three hundred foster children for almost thirty years. During that time, my dad served on church boards, as an elder, as an usher, as a youth pastor, and as a Sunday school teacher. My mom helped in every type of children's ministry, served as church secretary, and worked as a youth pastor, too.

We were far from rich, and things were often very tight, but I never saw an offering plate go by that they didn't drop something into, and I've never seen someone go hungry whom they knew about. They have always had enough surplus to be a blessing to others. After they retired from foster care, God blessed then with a large home on five acres. Mom really missed the kids, so my sisters and I agreed to fill their home with grandchildren...and now they have a surplus— ten under eight years old!

God has blessed my wife and me in so many ways. We truly live surplus lives! We have a surplus of close family members with whom we get together weekly, we have a surplus of four little girls, we have more friends at church than we can keep up with, and we've had a surplus of money for our entire married lives. In order to maintain surplus lives, we follow these three guidelines: test for kingdom purposes, pray to confirm, and give more than feels comfortable.

When we bought the home we are living in now, we knew it was much more than we needed. But as we walked through, visions of prayer meetings, church parties, and salvations in the living room filled our hearts! We knew it qualified for kingdom purpose, we prayed, and God confirmed, but this time, we gave less than what they were asking for the house—a lot less!

Surplus living seems to overlap in different areas for us. Recently, we were considering a ministry position at church, but I was concerned that it would be too much on top of trying to pilot our company through a terrible economy. We knew this qualified for kingdom purpose, but there would have to be confirmation through prayer. While I was praying, God reminded me whose company it really was. He told me that if we took the position at church, He would show me a miracle of finance and protect the company during the economic downturn.

The same month we accepted the position, the miracle started. We had a record profit for three months straight! These were months that typically didn't even have a profit. The miracle pulled us through a difficult year, and I'm believing for more surplus to come. We gave our time, and God dealt with the finances. When your overqualified CFO tells you that your company has a record profit but she doesn't exactly know how, you can be sure that the Holy Spirit has been working in accounting.

I think people who want to be surplus thinkers have to be guarded so that they don't start thinking it's all for them. I try not to take myself too seriously, or I might start giving of "my" surplus. I have done this before, and it's dangerous! The thing that has helped our family most in surplus living is remembering that it's all God's, anyway! For us, surplus boils down to stewardship—what surplus is God willing to entrust you with?

Yes to Surplus Resources

The surplus person progressively grows stronger and stronger in the power of the Holy Spirit, increasing the capacity and intensity

> *The surplus person progressively grows stronger and stronger in the power of the Holy Spirit.*

of the spiritual life. The surplus person also moves into a new level of believing and receiving God's supply of abundant resources, including finances. The surplus person has more than enough financial resources, which enables him or her to do the will of God, to reach out and fulfill the dreams that God has given, to bless others in need, to give liberally to the poor, and to bless the local church with tithes, offerings, and special financial gifts for missions to the nations. The surplus person believes the Scriptures about surplus resources.

Honor the LORD with your possessions, and with the firstfruits of all your increase; so your barns will be filled with plenty, and your vats will overflow with new wine. (Proverbs 3:9–10)

LORD, You will establish peace for us, for You have also done all our works in us. (Isaiah 26:12)

They will not be disgraced in hard times; even in famine they will have more than enough. (Psalm 37:19 NLT)

In hard times, they'll hold their heads high; when the shelves are bare, they'll be full. (Psalm 37:19 MSG)

In 1847, Ireland was in the midst of the Great Potato Famine, in which about one quarter of the population was lost—half of those to disease and famine, and half to emigration as people fled from starvation. In the United States, the Choctaw Indian tribe had just settled into new homes after being forced to leave their homeland and resettle in Oklahoma. Their journey has been called the Trail of Tears because of the thousands who died of starvation and disease on the trail. Living in a new land, building new homes and new lives, and learning to adapt to a new environment that was very different from their homeland meant that they were now living in times of need.

Yet when they heard about the famine in Ireland, the Choctaw refused to be shaped by the scarcity in which they lived. They would not be limited by the lack surrounding them. In the middle of their scarcity and lack, they took up a collection to give to the Irish. In the midst of their need, they gathered together 710 dollars to send to feed the starving men, women, and children in Ireland. In their lack, they maintained hearts of surplus and gave an amount that, in today's world, would be worth almost twenty thousand dollars.

Financial Resource Lack

Moving into a place of surplus resources necessitates understanding financial resource lack. *Lack* means "to be deficient or to have need of something that requires supply." Financial lack can be brought upon people by circumstances that are out of their control or circumstances that are rooted in geographical lack, poverty, or crisis. This can be seen in many nations of the world where famine, disease, and pestilence cause unbelievable poverty and lack.

Poverty is the deprivation of common necessities, such as food, clothing, shelter, and clean drinking water, all of which determine quality of life. *To lack* is to be deprived of those goods, services, and pleasures that others around us take for granted. Lack may affect individuals or groups, and it is not confined to developing nations. It can happen anywhere.

A person who is in lack of physical necessities may still have a surplus of spirit and soul. This can be seen all over the world. Those who have surplus resources have them in order to share with those who lack. When you consider the fact that 1.1 billion people live on less than one dollar per day and 2.7 billion people live on less than two dollars per day, the surplus in America becomes obvious. We have been blessed in order to be a blessing.

> *A person who is in lack of physical necessities may still have a surplus of spirit and soul.*

Resource lack can also be the result of living in a family environment that suffered financial pressures. You may be influenced by the unseen spirit of poverty or a poverty mentality. This is an attitude that sees lack as a way of life. This can and should be broken as you believe in God's Word and principles, which will bring blessing and

144 • *The Attitude of Faith*

abundance to your life. Your inheritance is not lack; it is surplus, abundant supply.

Financial lack can be the result of a person breaking the financial surplus principles as seen in the Scriptures. Breaking God's laws of finance will result in financial lack, in loss, and in a downward spiral that leads to a deep hole of debt, pressure, and living in lack. That is not God's will for you. Financial lack resulting in financial bondage negatively affects your relationships with God and others.

Financial lack can be the result of not understanding the principles set out by Scripture and by doing ignorant things that harm your finances. You may have "not enough" or "just enough" financial resources because of a lack of insight concerning surplus principles. The average household in America has a credit debt of eight thousand dollars, often forcing both spouses to work or one spouse to take on a second job. The result is often a lack of time and energy to build healthy relationships with each other or with the children.

If you will be openhearted and teachable, and if you will commit to God's idea of prosperity with a purpose, you can change your lack to more than enough.

Starting today, financial lack can be changed in your life. Say, "Yes, I am going to change from living in lack to living in surplus." If you will be openhearted and teachable, and if you will commit to God's idea of prosperity with a purpose, you can change your lack to more than enough. You can change your more than enough to surplus, and you can change your surplus to abundant overflow.

Pray the prayer for a new heart found in Ezekiel 36:26: *"I will give you a new heart and put a new spirit within you; I will take the heart of stone out of your flesh and give you a heart of flesh."* Believe that the old will pass away, as described in 2 Corinthians 5:17: *"If anyone is in Christ, he is a new creation; old things have passed away; behold, all things have become new."* And put on new knowledge, as described in Colossians 3:10: *"Put on the new man who is renewed in knowledge according to the image of Him who created him."*

Personal Testimony

Jeremy,
Missionary to Southeast Asia

One of my English students excitedly asked me, "Teacher, can I tell you what God did for me?" That's not a question to which you ever say no, so I sat down at the concrete table in the muggy Southeast Asian evening as the rest of the students partied indoors and listened as Noi began his story.

He talked about leaving his small village to come to the city, arriving with only the clothes he was wearing. He found a job selling bread that earned him just enough to buy his meal for each day. That was how he was living when I met him—one meal at a time. But Noi had been studying the Bible and had made an amazing discovery.

"Teacher, God is not mad at me if I have money. He wants me to work hard and to save money so I can help people." He pulled a small bank book out of his pocket, which was unheard of for a young man from a village. Few of them had ever been inside a bank, let alone had money to put into one. "Before, I only made enough for each day. Now, I sell more bread each day and make more money, so I can put money in the bank. Now, I have enough money to go back to my village and tell them about Jesus and teach them everything that I learn here."

He had more money in his possession than any of his friends or family could even dream have having. He could now get the things that he didn't have: new clothes, a new bicycle, or even a motorcycle. The list of what he didn't have was endless, but the list of where the money was going was short: a bus ticket twice a month that took him on an all-night ride up into the mountains, where he spent the next two days teaching Bible studies to the new believers, as well as to the not-yet believers, and then another all-night bus ride back to the city so he could start work the next morning.

Essential Components for Moving from Lack to Surplus

We must understand that surplus living does not happen overnight. It is a process requiring time and discipline with definite biblical components in place. You cannot break God's principles and then pray for a miracle like winning the lottery. You must build a house of surplus with the right materials to see surplus living. Financial bondage must be recognized, and you must break out of it.

Consistently worrying about money, borrowing from one lender to pay another so you can get by for an extra month, being unable to make your credit card payments and paying only interest, envying others who have enough money to do the things you want, not having a budget, constantly dreaming about get-rich-quick schemes—these are all signs of financial bondage. Breaking out of that bondage will take discipline. If you are not in bondage but are seeking to increase what you have, these components will work for you, as well.

Component 1: Stewardship

The careful and responsible management of what God has entrusted to your care is called *stewardship.* It involves your time, your strength, your talents, and your money. Luke 16:10 states, *"He who is faithful in what is least is faithful also in much; and he who is unjust in what is least is unjust also in much."* Stewardship is an act of worship that recognizes God as the owner of all things, doing everything with His objectives, His interests, and His glorification in mind.

> *Stewardship is an act of worship that recognizes God as the owner of all things.*

J. L. Kraft, head of the Kraft Cheese Corporation, gave approximately 25 percent of his income to Christian causes for many years. He has been widely reported as saying, "The only investment I ever made that has paid consistently increasing dividends is the money I have given to the Lord."

The financial principles in the Word of God are there because God knows they are the best ways for us to use our money. God's principles of finance are not an arbitrary set of rules to govern us.

They are a loving Father's wisdom to those who will listen to and trust Him. Stewardship believes that God owns everything, that God created everything, and that God releases everything. It all comes from Him. Saint Augustine said,

> Find out how much God has given you and from it take what you need. The remainder which you do not require is needed by others. The extras of the rich are the necessities of the poor. Those who retain what is superfluous possess the goods of others.[22]

When material things start possessing us, God is moved to the periphery of our lives, and the things we want to possess prohibit our spiritual growth. Jesus said it very simply: *"For where your treasure is, there your heart will be also"* (Matthew 6:21). How distressing it is to find that the things we earnestly pursued and believed we needed for our welfare, once attained, turn out to be the cause of growing emptiness.

Component 2: Working

God has called every person to be a good and skilled worker. Working with diligence and integrity is biblical, and God promises to reward hard work.

> *Bondservants, obey in all things your masters according to the flesh, not with eyeservice, as men-pleasers, but in sincerity of heart, fearing God. And whatever you do, do it heartily, as to the Lord and not to men, knowing that from the Lord you will receive the reward of the inheritance; for you serve the Lord Christ.*
> (Colossians 3:22–24)

> *Wealth gained by dishonesty will be diminished, but he who gathers by labor will increase.* (Proverbs 13:11)

This is a great time for hard and honest workers to excel at their jobs. Finding good employees is crucial to businesses. The better the employees, the more likely that a company will be successful. Bad employees can cost businesses incredible amounts of time, resources, and money. Characteristics of the ideal worker include dependability, honesty, integrity, positivity, productivity, punctuality, being proactive and hardworking, following instructions, being cooperative and getting along with other workers, being conscientious about break times, and being a team player.

If you are to live a surplus life, you will need to put this link in the chain: the *absolute surplus* link. Do your best work for your company. Be an example of a true worker. Be proactive; go after things instead of waiting for them to come to you.

Your work attitude projects your beliefs and values and communicates what you think about your job, your coworkers, and your boss. Be a positive worker with a positive attitude. This does not necessarily mean that you will always be happy, but it means that you maintain a right attitude even in difficult situations. In 1 Timothy 6:1–3, Paul challenged employees, saying,

> *Let as many bondservants as are under the yoke count their own masters worthy of all honor, so that the name of God and His doctrine may not be blasphemed. And those who have believing masters, let them not despise them because they are brethren, but rather serve them because those who are benefited are believers and beloved. Teach and exhort these things. If anyone teaches otherwise and does not consent to wholesome words, even the words of our Lord Jesus Christ, and to the doctrine which accords with godliness.*

The Bible promises promotion, blessing, favor, and prosperity to the hard worker who serves with diligence, honesty, and skill. Proverbs 22:29 notes, *"Do you see a man who excels in his work? He will stand before kings; he will not stand before unknown men."* Be an employee of excellence, and you will stand out.

Component 3: Giving

Giving of your resources, beginning with tithes and offerings to the church in which God has placed you, activates the divine law that releases the blessings of God into your personal life. The first step toward building this link into the chain of surplus living is learning to give your tithe. The tithe is simply the tenth part of something, paid as a voluntary contribution. It is called *"the first-fruits,"* or the first part of our income. It is sacred to God. Proverbs 3:9 says, *"Honor the LORD with your possessions, and with the firstfruits of all your increase."*

You are to take the first part of your income, earnings, or profits and cheerfully give to God, as He is your Partner who works on your behalf. God has given mankind the exclusive right or dominion to rule over His property and world. We have not only been given the right of dominion, but we are also free moral agents, able to make our own decisions and determine our own actions.

Therefore, a person can either bless or curse God with his or her actions. Obedience blesses God, while disobedience is a reproach to God. Tithing blesses. It is an act of honor and faith in God's Word. We know that God owns everything. *"The earth is the LORD's, and all its fullness, the world and those who dwell therein"* (Psalm 24:1). God

> *Obedience blesses God, while disobedience is a reproach to God.*

declares that all resources are His. *"'The silver is Mine, and the gold is Mine,' says the LORD of hosts"* (Haggai 2:8). God owns everything, and we are stewards of His possessions.

Surplus living will not happen without every component in place, including liberal giving that believes for surplus resources to be poured out upon your life, as promised by God.

> *"Bring all the tithes into the storehouse, that there may be food in My house, and try Me now in this," says the LORD of hosts, "If I will not open for you the windows of heaven and pour out for you such blessing that there will not be room enough to receive it. And I will rebuke the devourer for your sakes, so that he will not destroy the fruit of your ground, nor shall the vine fail to bear fruit for you in the field," says the LORD of hosts.*
> (Malachi 3:10–11)

You should not only give your tithe, but you should also give your offering, which is a voluntary, unlimited amount presented by the giver with faith and joy. The faith to be a great giver with a great giver's heart is the goal. Be generous. Be liberal. Be ready to bless others. Tithe is always 10 percent, but offerings are unlimited, Spirit-led, and cheerfully given.

God's Word declares, *"So let each one give as he purposes in his heart, not grudgingly or of necessity; for God loves a cheerful giver"* (2 Corinthians 9:7). A faith-giver believes God to be a good God, a God of abundance, and an all-things-are-possible God. Proverbs 11:24–26 lays out the principle of God rewarding the generous:

> *There is one who scatters, yet increases more; and there is one who withholds more than is right, but it leads to poverty. The generous soul will be made rich, and he who waters will also be watered himself. The people will curse him who withholds grain, but blessing will be on the head of him who sells it.*

Component 4: Receiving

God responds to our giving by opening up opportunities for us to receive divine provision—both directly and indirectly—from the hand of God. Surplus living involves surplus receiving.

> *Give, and it will be given to you: good measure, pressed down, shaken together, and running over will be put into your bosom. For with the same measure that you use, it will be measured back to you.* (Luke 6:38)

Notice that it says, *"and it will be given to you."* This is the promise of receiving what God desires to pour into your life. Receiving is a biblical faith position and is a key to surplus flow. Matthew 7:8 promises, *"For everyone who asks receives, and he who seeks finds, and to him who knocks it will be opened."* In Mark 10:30, Jesus declared that those who forsake everything to follow Him will *"receive a hundredfold now in this time; houses and brothers and sisters and mothers and children and lands, with persecutions; and in the age to come, eternal life."*

If you were a farmer sowing seed, you would believe that the harvest was coming and that there would be a reward—reaping, receiving, fulfillment. All seed will produce more than what is planted, and so it is in God's economy. We plant, and God gives the increase. There must be a mind-set to receive, a faith expectation that believes you will receive your full portion. Come to God with open hands and open hearts, prayerfully obtaining what God chooses to pour into them. Scripture says that those who ask will receive, so ask! Receive! Receive increase, blessing, favor, multiplication, and miracles. Pray Jabez' prayer:

> *Come to God with open hands and open hearts, prayerfully obtaining what God chooses to pour into them.*

> *Now Jabez was more honorable than his brothers, and his mother called his name Jabez, saying, "Because I bore him in pain." And Jabez called on the God of Israel saying, "Oh, that You would bless me indeed, and enlarge my territory, that Your hand would be with me, and that You would keep me from evil, that I may not cause pain!" So God granted him what he requested.* (1 Chronicles 4:9–10)

Believe that God desires to bless you. Desire to receive that you may be a blessing.

> *So he gave them his attention, expecting to receive something from them.* (Acts 3:5)

> *He shall receive blessing from the LORD, and righteousness from the God of his salvation.* (Psalm 24:5)

> *Until now you have asked nothing in My name. Ask, and you will receive, that your joy may be full.* (John 16:24)

Receive with open hands. Take it. Hold on to it. Make room for what is coming to you. The attitude of receiving is to take and receive by faith with open hands, making room for and receiving by deliberate and ready reception all that God is bringing into your hands. Receive from your work or business. Receive from wise decisions and investments. Receive from surprise blessings.

Believe Psalm 84:11: *"For the LORD God is a sun and shield; the LORD will give grace and glory; no good thing will He withhold from those who walk uprightly."* This promise is one that should stay before your eyes on a daily basis. The Lord our God is a good God, a God who does not withhold, and a God who enjoys releasing good things into our lives.

Component 5: Managing

Surplus living necessitates managing all the blessings of God upon your life.

Surplus living necessitates managing all the blessings of God upon your life. God expects and requires believers to manage their lives biblically—including their money. Managing your resources by biblical principles allows God to bless you and bless other people through you. God evaluates you as a servant who is using His resources, not as an owner using your own resources.

God is interested in the quality of financial management, not just the quantity of the finances managed. Godly, biblical money management is a matter of *how* and not of *how much*. Managing your resources means having an attitude of dependence on the Lord and trusting Him totally. God desires that you should enjoy your life, your blessings, and all that He puts into your hands.

When John G. Wendel and his sisters received a huge inheritance from their parents, they opted for an aggressive saving type of money management. They spent as little as they could and hoarded the rest. John was able to keep the money from being split up by convincing five of his six sisters never to get married. For fifty years, they lived in the same house in New York City, saving every penny. When the final sister died in 1931, she was worth one hundred million dollars. Yet, even with all that money, she owned only one dress, which she had made for herself twenty-five years earlier. They managed their resources unbiblically, depending only on themselves, living in fear, not trusting the Lord, and not being a source of blessing to others.

His lord said to him, "Well done, good and faithful servant; you were faithful over a few things, I will make you ruler over many things. Enter into the joy of your lord."   (Matthew 25:21)

This verse shows us the attitude associated with godly money management. Managing your finances in a godly way means living wisely and frugally in all things. It means living with contentment, and it means living more simply than our culture dictates. It means finding joy and satisfaction more in relationships and simple pleasures and less in the things the world tells us we must have.

Surplus living is wise living, and wisely managing what you have will determine how much God can pour into your hands. If you do not learn to manage your money, it will manage you. Maintain good financial records. Be attentive to what you own, what you owe, what you earn, and where it goes. Plan your spending. Maintain good budgeting. These habits lead to surplus living and allow you to have more than enough. There is nothing immoral about possessing money or material goods—it is how that money is used that is an expression of the spiritual lives of believers.

Component 6: Prospering

God desires that we receive abundantly and have more than enough so that we can bless others and become liberal givers. Our prayer should be that of Psalm 118:25: *"Save now, I pray, O LORD; O LORD, I pray, send now prosperity."* Pray 3 John 2: *"Beloved, I pray that you may prosper in all things and be in health, just as your soul prospers."*

Prosperity is a successful, flourishing, or thriving condition in all aspects of life—spiritual, emotional, domestic, relational, and financial.

If they obey and serve Him, they shall spend their days in prosperity, and their years in pleasures. (Job 36:11)

He himself shall dwell in prosperity, and his descendants shall inherit the earth. (Psalm 25:13)

Honor the LORD with your possessions, and with the firstfruits of all your increase; so your barns will be filled with plenty, and your vats will overflow with new wine. (Proverbs 3:9–10)

Prosperity begins with your decision to believe that God desires to use you to bless others and that to do so means you must have

> *Prosperity begins with your decision to believe that God desires to use you to bless others.*

more than enough—you must have an overflow, a surplus, an abundance. You must have unwavering faith in God, confidence in your ability to live your dreams, and courage to overcome anything that stands between you and those dreams. Surplus living should be one of your dreams—to prosper with a purpose and fulfill a mission.

Throw off the constraints and limitations that you have allowed to choke your progress. Prosperous people live with clarity, not confusion. You are absolutely clear about who you are in Christ, what you are called to do, and where you are going. You never stop learning, growing, changing, and achieving. You progress consistently to become all that God has called you to be. Concentrate on the greatness of God and on His promises to you. Be single-minded in your pursuits, and stick with your dreams until they are fulfilled.

Prosperity with a purpose begins when you challenge your attitude and thoughts. The surplus person realizes that the universe is full of abundance and that whatever he or she needs to fulfill his or her purpose is already available. Surplus living begins with the belief that God has made it possible for you to prosper. Pray the following prayer.

Lord, today I surrender my whole life into Your hands, including my financial affairs and my concerns about my money, resources, job, and business. Lord, remove my worries and fears about the future and replace them with faith. I ask that You would make my purpose clear and my pathway blessed by Your provisions. Amen.

The surplus life that you are called to is a true and attainable life. God wants you to be successful in everything you do and to be raised with great honor to receive the promotion prepared for you. Surplus living is a gradual journey; it avoids the extremes that damage biblical values, homes, health, relationships, and character. True surplus living is found where balanced living has been achieved.

Chapter 8

Yes to Fulfilling Dreams

When I was eighteen, I had no real direction in my life, although I had lots of options and ideas for myself, and other people had lots of ideas and counsel for me. I had already taken some steps to point my life in the right direction: I had taken an aptitude test, done a career search to find in-demand jobs, and written out my wish list of what I would do if I could have any job I wanted.

I knew that I did not want any of the careers I had investigated. I wanted to play semi-pro baseball or maybe even make it to the big leagues. Yes, that was a great plan! I wanted a life of playing the sport I loved, and I was confident that I could do it if I just had the chance. I spoke with my friends and coaches and received a lot of encouragement to pursue that option.

And pursue it I did. I and two hundred other dreamers went to a UCLA open field tryout for the Kansas City Royals. I hung in there, cut after cut, until there were only a few players left. At that final cut, they chose one person, and I was not it. I will never forget the man who broke the news. He lined the fifteen of us up on the grass and faced us. We looked nervously at his old, wrinkled face as he shifted the chaw in his mouth. "Boys," he said in slow, deliberate speech, "you are not good enough for pro ball. Find a good job in another career, because baseball isn't it."

I walked away completely discouraged and a little angry that he had missed my hidden greatness and not signed me for the future! That was one of the most significant days of my life. I shut the door to that dream and opened the door to new possibilities. I wondered,

If this is the only thing that has been on my heart to do, and this was not it, what could there be that I have not yet discovered? It was my wake-up call—my time to find out what should drive my life into the future.

The dreams of the heart are placed there as dreams of faith, things hoped for and prayed for, and things you give your life to. Dreams can be out of your reach but still burn in the deepest recesses of your heart. You may have had a dream since childhood that no one else knows about. A dream may be a passion of your heart to go or to do certain things.

What are the dreams of your heart? What dreams have died in you and need to be revived? What dreams have fallen to the ground and need to be picked up? What would you do with your life, or attempt to do, if you knew it was impossible to fail? What goal has God placed into your heart that He desires you to fulfill? Allow the Holy Spirit to expand your thoughts about your future. Not everything you dream will be a dream of God, and even some of the dreams of God may not happen the way you think they will. God begins every dream with a seed thought tucked away deep in your heart as an invisible idea that gives birth to a visible, tangible reality.

When the baseball dream fell to the ground, it was a pivotal turning point for me; but another dream was already taking root in my heart. I did not realize the full potential of that seed. Looking back now, it is hard to imagine that I could have done with my life anything other than what I am doing now and have been doing for over four decades. The dream that captured my heart was not mine; it was a God-dream. God knows me better than anyone else, so it is understandable that He would be the dream-Giver and I would be the dream-receiver.

> *God is the dream-Giver, and I am the dream-receiver.*

Stop for a moment and absorb that thought: *God is the dream-Giver, and I am the dream-receiver.* It is not up to you to be the architect of your life, your future, and your dreams. God is the dream-Architect, and He knows exactly what your dream should look like. You can turn your heart over to God and allow Him to fill it with

His dream, knowing He is a loving and good God who has only your best interests in His will and mind.

When you know this and trust God for a dream encounter, life takes on the joyful, new adventure of letting go and letting God take control. God desires to encounter you in a very real and life-changing experience. It is the God-way. He initiates, He involves our lives, and He takes us to places in life where we will encounter Him.

Personal Testimony

Joel,
Missionary to Japan in His Thirties with
a Wife and Three Children

I was born and raised in Japan in a missionary family. As a teenager, I had absolutely no desire to go into the ministry like my parents and two older brothers before me. However, that all changed when our family was on furlough in 1988. I was sixteen and attending the youth camp of Bible Temple (now City Bible Church) in Portland, Oregon. During an evening meeting, the speaker made an altar call for those who felt like they were supposed to go into ministry. I immediately discounted the altar call. The speaker made another appeal, and suddenly, my heart began to pound. I didn't want to go up, but I was scared of the consequences of not responding, so I prayed a quick prayer: "God, You know I don't want to go into the ministry, but if this is You, I will go up in faith."

As I went forward, I had one of the most powerful encounters with God that I have ever had. He spoke to me through a vision in which I saw myself standing over Japan and holding a Bible in my hand. I responded in faith, and God spoke to me about my future, changing my heart forever.

I can still see that vision today as clearly as I saw it in 1988. Ever since that experience, everything I did was based on going back to Japan. I graduated from Bible college, married a girl with a heart for Japan, and served in City Bible Church until 2007, when God very specifically opened the door to go to Japan.

God used that vision to lead me through every difficult situation, every desert experience, and every major decision I made. It would not let me go. Each time I took the step of faith toward the vision, God was always faithful to lead and provide. Twenty-one years after my encounter with God, we planted a church in Osaka, Japan. God was very specific in His calling, preparation, sending, and fulfillment, but the only requirement on my part was to respond in faith. There is nothing more rewarding than knowing that you are in the right place, at the right time, in the middle of God's will!

People in Scripture Who Had God-Encounters

Jacob

Now Jacob went out from Beersheba and went toward Haran. So he came to a certain place and stayed there all night, because the sun had set. And he took one of the stones of that place and put it at his head, and he lay down in that place to sleep. Then he dreamed, and behold, a ladder was set up on the earth, and its top reached to heaven; and there the angels of God were ascending and descending on it. And behold, the Lord stood above it and said: "I am the Lord God of Abraham your father and the God of Isaac; the land on which you lie I will give to you and your descendants. Also your descendants shall be as the dust of the earth; you shall spread abroad to the west and the east, to the north and the south; and in you and in your seed all the families of the earth shall be blessed. Behold, I am with you and will keep you wherever you go, and will bring you back to this land; for I will not leave you until I have done what I have spoken to you."
(Genesis 28:10–15)

Joseph

Now Joseph had a dream, and he told it to his brothers; and they hated him even more. So he said to them, "Please hear this dream

which I have dreamed: There we were, binding sheaves in the field. Then behold, my sheaf arose and also stood upright; and indeed your sheaves stood all around and bowed down to my sheaf."
(Genesis 37:5–7)

Now Joseph was governor over the land; and it was he who sold to all the people of the land. And Joseph's brothers came and bowed down before him with their faces to the earth. (Genesis 42:6)

Joshua

This Book of the Law shall not depart from your mouth, but you shall meditate in it day and night, that you may observe to do according to all that is written in it. For then you will make your way prosperous, and then you will have good success.
(Joshua 1:8)

Gideon

Then the Lord turned to him and said, "Go in this might of yours, and you shall save Israel from the hand of the Midianites. Have I not sent you?" (Judges 6:14)

Esther

For if you remain completely silent at this time, relief and deliverance will arise for the Jews from another place, but you and your father's house will perish. Yet who knows whether you have come to the kingdom for such a time as this? (Esther 4:14)

David

So he sent and brought him in. Now he was ruddy, with bright eyes, and good-looking. And the LORD said, "Arise, anoint him; for this is the one!" Then Samuel took the horn of oil and anointed him in the midst of his brothers; and the Spirit of the LORD came upon David from that day forward. So Samuel arose and went to Ramah.
(1 Samuel 16:12–13)

Jeremiah

Before I formed you in the womb I knew you; before you were born I sanctified you; I ordained you a prophet to the nations.
(Jeremiah 1:5)

Ananias

Now there was a certain disciple at Damascus named Ananias; and to him the Lord said in a vision, "Ananias." And he said, "Here I am, Lord." So the Lord said to him, "Arise and go to the street called Straight, and inquire at the house of Judas for one called Saul of Tarsus, for behold, he is praying. And in a vision he has seen a man named Ananias coming in and putting his hand on him, so that he might receive his sight."
(Acts 9:10–12)

Paul

Therefore, King Agrippa, I was not disobedient to the heavenly vision.
(Acts 26:19)

A vision appeared to Paul in the night. A man of Macedonia stood and pleaded with him, saying, "Come over to Macedonia and help us." Now after he had seen the vision, immediately we sought to go to Macedonia, concluding that the Lord had called us to preach the gospel to them.
(Acts 16:9–10)

Now the Lord spoke to Paul in the night by a vision, "Do not be afraid, but speak, and do not keep silent."
(Acts 18:9)

Peter

Jesus, walking by the Sea of Galilee, saw two brothers, Simon called Peter, and Andrew his brother, casting a net into the sea; for they were fishermen. Then He said to them, "Follow Me, and I will make you fishers of men." They immediately left their nets and followed Him.
(Matthew 4:18–20)

Dreams Come in a God-Encounter

The God-encounter is a vital part of receiving the dreams that God has for you. God will give the dream. It is a seed word or a picture that is planted deep in your heart to grow and bear fruit. The dream is that future hope or desire that will remain in your heart. It is a picture of the future that puts fire in your heart and saturates your soul. It is the faith to see what can become reality when God is your Partner and dream-Giver.

Jeremiah 29:11 says, *"For I know the thoughts that I think toward you, says the LORD, thoughts of peace and not of evil, to give you a future and a hope."* God will help you discern His thoughts, His dream, and His will for your life. God's dreams are far greater than our dreams.

"For My thoughts are not your thoughts, nor are your ways My ways," says the LORD. "For as the heavens are higher than the earth, so are My ways higher than your ways, and My thoughts than your thoughts.
(Isaiah 55:8–9)

> The God-encounter is a vital part of receiving the dreams that God has for you.

When the God-encounter takes place, you will know it. It could be a time when you prepare to meet with God through dedicated fasting and prayer, solitude, and waiting on the Lord. It could be a time of crisis when you hit the wall and give up—a time of total darkness in a deep valley—before God enters that moment with a new dream for your life. It could be that you are going about your daily business (working at your job, cleaning your house, sitting in class at school) or that you are stepping out into a new venture (getting married, having your first child, moving to a new city) and something happens inside you.

When this happens, it may be imperceptible at first—a faint voice in your soul, a deep desire, a feeling, or an idea. Then, it will begin to make itself known, growing stronger every day until you face it head-on and realize that God is there in a new and unique way. You will know that you are experiencing a God-encounter. Like what happened to Paul in Acts 9:18, the scales will fall from your eyes, and they will be opened to see something you have not seen before.

Dreams Develop through the God-Encounter

Perhaps your vision will come slowly, as it did for the blind man in Mark 8:22–25:

> Then He came to Bethsaida; and they brought a blind man to Him, and begged Him to touch him. So He took the blind man by the hand and led him out of the town. And when He had spit on his eyes and put His hands on him, He asked him if he saw anything. And he looked up and said, "I see men like trees, walking." Then He put His hands on his eyes again and made him look up. And he was restored and saw everyone clearly.

You may see only dimly at first, but with one more touch from God, you will clearly see the dream, and the hidden springs of your heart will burst forth.

Destiny Is Unveiled in the God-Encounter

When you encounter God and know for sure that He has done something in you and has opened up something for you, there is a new sense of destiny. Your life has a God-appointment upon it—a reason for living and going through any and all trials and tests in life. All the excuses from the past will fall away from your life like the leaves falling off the trees in autumn. They will release their holds on your life and drift to the ground to die. You will no longer be ruled by excuses like the following:

- *I don't have what it takes to do those kinds of things.*
- *I don't have the motivation to rise to such great dreams.*
- *I don't have the skills, talents, or training to make this happen.*
- *I don't know if I could make the sacrifices to do what I desire to do.*
- *I don't want the responsibility of success.*
- *I lack the strength and energy for this dream.*
- *I am too old.*
- *I am too young.*
- *I do not have enough money or resources.*

All these excuses will lie in cast-off piles around your life. When you encounter God, all of these excuses will mean nothing to you anymore. God is on your side, and He will give you all that you need to achieve the God-dream for your life. Believe Matthew 19:26: *"Jesus looked at them and said to them, 'With men this is impossible, but with God all things are possible.'"*

> *God is on your side, and He will give you all that you need to achieve the God-dream for your life.*

There is a little book called *Every Excuse in the Book: 714 Ways to Say "It's Not My Fault!"* In the section labeled "I Could've Been Somebody But...," the authors list common excuses, some of which are:

- I was a day-care baby.
- I was an underprivileged child.
- My mom used to walk me on a leash.
- It's a male-dominated world.
- My parents always liked my brother best.
- I was raised by wolves.
- It was predestination.
- I had no choice.
- I ate too much junk food.
- I've been through a lot.
- Dear Abby steered me wrong.
- I have low self-esteem.
- I'm messed up from reading self-help books.
- The psychic network lied to me.
- I come from bad stock.
- I was caught up in forces I don't understand.
- I drank milk after the expiration date.[23]

When my baseball dream fell to the ground, God encountered me with His Word and His Spirit. Through other people's prayers for me and time spent with God, I had a real, spiritual encounter that gave me the thoughts of God to set my course for life. The dream seeds were deep inside my heart, but it took the watering of the Holy Spirit to break open the seed and cause it to grow.

Personal Testimony

Melissa,
Single Woman in Her Twenties

It was on a mission trip to India when I first got a glimpse of God's heart and a vision that has consumed my life ever since. I was surrounded by hopeless, poor people and naked children begging for money on the streets of Delhi when I prayed this prayer: "Lord, give me Your heart." A reply came to my spirit like a bolt of lightning: "You can't handle My heart." I could almost see the sorrow God felt for all the people He loved who were going to hell. It ruined me. I told God that from that point on, I wanted to dedicate my life to helping people know about His redemptive love.

When I came back to the States, I got involved in Stitches Bible Club, a bus outreach at my church. The more I got into it, the bigger my vision grew. I wasn't just satisfied with kids knowing Jesus; I wanted to see teenagers and adults know Jesus and become integral parts of the church. I began to write down my vision of what that would look like. In my vision, I saw more buses bringing in kids from low-income apartments every Sunday. I saw people from the church picking up at-risk teens for youth services so they could experience the presence of God. I saw sports outreaches on weekends pull teens from the community into the church. I saw parents being helped by existing ministries like ESL, All Things New, and Financial Peace University.

Over the past nine years, this vision has unfolded, and I have seen hundreds of children from Buddhist, Catholic, or various broken backgrounds make Jesus their Lord and Savior. I have seen messed up and confused teens flood the altars, where God has met them. I have seen them baptized, wanting to start Bible studies in their schools, and desiring to bring their friends to church so that they can also experience the presence of God. I saw a lady who had been abused her whole life and who had turned to a homosexual lifestyle surrender her life to Christ and be restored in the All Things New class.

We started an ESL class at one of the apartment complexes where many of the parents lived. We are reaching more and more youth from the community through our monthly sports outreach. I have seen God show His miraculous power by growing back a little boy's finger right in front of his Buddhist father. Teens are now telling me that they want to go on mission trips, and one boy named Theo said he wants to start a Stitches program in Africa with me someday. God has exceeded my expectations, yet I'm still not satisfied. I know that there are many more souls to reach, so it's time to dream again, write the vision even bigger, and see God do even greater things.

Melissa is now serving in a staff position at her church because Stitches grew so large that it required a full-time employee.

The Power of a Dream Seed

Dream seeds are as powerful as natural seeds. In a seed lies the fierce force of life that will develop unseen by anyone outside. Seeds are not passive; they are one of nature's mighty miracles. The great redwood tree, which grows approximately 375 feet tall and twenty feet wide, comes from a seed that is one-sixteenth of an inch long. The size of the seed has no relationship to the size of the plant or tree that develops from it. The seed God has placed in you may be small and undetected until the God-encounter, but it is there, it will grow, and you will fulfill the God-dream.

One of the great encouragers in my life gave me a poem at a point when I was just beginning to see the dream. Something was shifting in me and struggling to get out. It was the God-dream. She gave me the following words, written by Edwin Markham, and I have carried them in my wallet for more than twenty years.

> Ah, great it is to believe the dream
> As we stand in youth by the starry stream;
> But a greater thing is to fight live life through,
> And say in the end, "The dream is true!"

The seed of God's call on my life to pastor, preach, teach, write, and train leaders was in the birthing process, but it needed to grow. Every seed needs the right environment for it to grow. It must have the right soil, be planted at the right depth, and be given the proper care. Seeds have an intricate mechanism that determines the right time and the right place for sprouting. If all the pieces are not in place, a seed cannot sprout.

Four Locks on the Dream Seed

There are four locks that must be opened before the seed will break ground.

1. The first is the **water** lock. If a seed has no water, it will dry out and remain locked in the earth. When water penetrates the seed, unstoppable change begins.

2. The second is the **oxygen** lock. The breath of life is in the oxygen, and a seed must have that breath for life to spring forth.

3. The third lock is **temperature**. If it is either too cold or too hot, the seed can be destroyed or kept dormant. Balanced warmth opens the seed for growth.

4. Finally, there is the **light** lock. Light tells the seed it is near enough to the soil's surface to emerge and break ground. Darkness affects the seed, causing it to die or lie dormant in the ground for years.

God's plan is for the seed to break through these locks and bring about a great harvest.

> *For the seed shall be prosperous, the vine shall give its fruit, the ground shall give her increase, and the heavens shall give their dew; I will cause the remnant of this people to possess all these.*
> (Zechariah 8:12)

The God-encounter will help to clarify the dream, and it will also water the seed. God desires to appear—to reveal Himself—to you in a life-changing way. In 1 Kings 3:5, God appeared to Solomon in a dream at night and asked, *"What shall I give you?"* God wants to come to you with the same question: *"What shall I give you?"* He comes to plant the seed of a dream in your heart and then water it to bring it to full growth.

> *God comes to plant the seed of a dream in your heart and then water it to bring it to full growth.*

The language of the Holy Spirit is the language of dreams and visions. It is the power to imagine—the power to see the God-idea. The Holy Spirit will help you form a vivid and powerful image of something not yet experienced by your natural senses. To dream is to see with the eyes of the heart, causing anticipation and expectation that fix your eyes on a God-mark.

We do not look at the things which are seen, but at the things which are not seen. For the things which are seen are temporary, but the things which are not seen are eternal.
(2 Corinthians 4:18)

Dreams Give You a Future

A person without a dream is a person without a future, and a person without a future will always return to his or her past. Dreams give you a future. They make you achieve faith goals, reach higher, and go further in life. Choose the imperishable, see the invisible, and do the impossible. Do not settle for less, for a smaller dream, or for an easier road to take. Go for the God-encounter with a God-dream and finish your race, having lived for the eternal and not the temporal.

You have the capacity to dream. You have the ability to dream. You are a dreamer in the making. Desire with a strong passion that the dream will become reality in your life. Fuel your dream with prayer. Visualize what God is saying to you with the clear picture He has given you. Associate yourself with other dreamers

168 • The Attitude of Faith

and absorb their spirit of faith, vision, courage, and endurance. Stay away from the faithless, negative, small-minded people who drain you of belief in the power of the dream. Concentrate. Focus. Stay on target. Imagine the dream coming to fulfillment. See it. Pray it. Say it. Declare it.

Great achievers usually have learned to replay the pictures of their past victories and pre-play the pictures of their future victories. David replayed his triumphs over the bear and lion as he faced his new challenge with Goliath. (See 1 Samuel 17:34–37.) Set your dream before your eyes. Think only on things that build up your spirit. (See Philippians 4:8.) Do not let your mind be filled with negative strongholds; clean your mind out and pull down all the strongholds. (See 2 Corinthians 10:5.)

> *A dreamer is one who sees the future as if it were already here.*

A dreamer is one who sees the future as if it were already here. A dreamer is not one who is content to live within the natural realm alone. A dreamer overcomes all that is necessary to finish the dream, bringing it to completion and ending the course successfully.

Since we are surrounded by so great a cloud of witnesses, let us lay aside every weight, and the sin which so easily ensnares us, and let us run with endurance the race that is set before us.
(Hebrews 12:1)

Personal Testimony

Ben,
Late Twenties, Married with an Infant;
Pastor of Lifeplace in Brisbane, Australia

For years, I had the desire in my heart to plant a church in Australia. I never knew that the process of preparation would take me to the other side of the world to learn from

Pastor Frank Damazio. I remember that my wife and I were in Sydney, staying with a friend for a few days before flying to Los Angeles. We had sold everything, put our clothes into six suitcases, and were en route to Portland. We left friends, family, and security to pursue our dream.

One night, this friend took us down to a cliff that overlooked the ocean off the Northern Beaches of Sydney. There was a full moon, and you could see the golden reflection rippling in the dark water below. We looked out, and he pointed to the horizon. He said, "You have to leave the harbor to reach the horizon." We were nervous, but in our hearts, we said yes to the dream.

After three amazing years, we were sent back to plant a church in Australia and see the dream unfold. Trying to plant a church and fund-raise amid the worst financial crises in history was not easy. I thought I was crazy at times! But we made a choice to step out in expectation, and God did the rest. God provided in so many ways. Now, we are back in Australia, we are pioneering a church, and what was once just a seed of expectation in our hearts is now a growing reality.

The Commitments of a Dream Finisher

King David was a dreamer and a finisher of His God-given dreams. In 1 Chronicles 28:20, he gave his son Solomon eight *finisher* commitments that a dream finisher must do in order to finish strong.

David said to his son Solomon, "Be strong and of good courage, and do it; do not fear nor be dismayed, for the LORD God; my God; will be with you. He will not leave you nor forsake you, until you have finished all the work for the service of the house of the LORD."

The Message Bible says it this way:

David continued to address Solomon: "Take charge! Take heart! Don't be anxious or get discouraged. GOD, my God, is with you in this; he won't walk off and leave you in the lurch. He's at your side until every last detail is completed for conducting the worship of GOD."

1. Take hold of the dream with a strong hand.

[My] *son Solomon, "Be strong."*

The dreamer must seize, or take hold of, the dream with a strong hand. To *take hold* is to be determined to do whatever is necessary for the dream to be fulfilled. The strength to take hold of the God-dream is in the strength and power of God's enabling Holy Spirit in your life. It is taking hold of God's ability, which is available to you, and taking hold of God's resources, grace, power, and supernatural provision. Taking hold does not mean that I will do the dream by my superior power; I will do it by faith in God's power in me and by laying claim to the promises in Scripture. (See also 1 Chronicles 22:13; 2 Chronicles 32:7; Haggai 2:4; Zechariah 8:9.)

> *The strength to take hold of the God-dream is the power of the Holy Spirit in your life.*

Fear not, for I am with you; be not dismayed, for I am your God. I will strengthen you, yes, I will help you, I will uphold you with My righteous right hand. (Isaiah 41:10)

This is the word of the LORD to Zerubbabel: "Not by might nor by power, but by My Spirit," says the LORD of hosts. "Who are you, O great mountain? Before Zerubbabel you shall become a plain! And he shall bring forth the capstone with shouts of 'Grace, grace to it!'" (Zechariah 4:6–7)

Not by might. Not by the influence of my hands. Not by the things that exist now, or by the visible wealth around me. Not by my power. I can stand before a target with bow in hand and pull the bow to the utmost of my strength. I can feel as if it is stretched to its maximum capacity, yet when I release the bowstring, the arrow does not have the power to reach the target.

In life, I can stand before the challenge and yet not have the strength needed to meet it. I do not have the power to hit the target without that extra power from the Holy Spirit. He puts His hands on my hands and pulls the bowstring back. The strength to take hold is in the power of God, not in the strength of man.

2. Regain your strength and take aggressive action today.

"Be...of good courage, and do it."

When King David gave these words to his son Solomon, the challenge was great. The dream was only a thought—a God-idea. The temple had not been built, and all the resources required were not yet available. David's word to a dreamer was to find his place of courage and move ahead to fulfill the dream.

The building of the *Beit Hamikdah*, as it was named in Hebrew, was called the "first temple." This had never been done before. The dream was to build the first of something for the people of God. Has God called you to build a first of something? Something new? Something never done before? This new thing may be the first ever to happen in your life, your family, or your family tree. Has God put a *first* dream in your heart? Take courage! Rise up and do it! Solomon went on to become the king with the greatest wealth, wisdom, and power. He did all that the dream demanded.

To *be of good courage* means to be bold, to be alert, and to grow stronger and stronger as you face any and all dream challenges. Psalm 27:14 says, *"Wait on the LORD; be of good courage, and He shall strengthen your heart; wait, I say, on the LORD!"* Psalm 31:24 repeats, *"Be of good courage, and He shall strengthen your heart, all you who hope in the LORD."* The quality of being filled up with courage is necessary for every dreamer, as God told Joshua:

> *Only be strong and very courageous, that you may observe to do according to all the law which Moses My servant commanded you; do not turn from it to the right hand or to the left, that you may prosper wherever you go.*   (Joshua 1:7)

> *You must have a holy stubbornness to stand your ground in faith and do what God has put into your heart.*

You must have a holy stubbornness to stand your ground in faith and do what God has put into your heart. There is no problem or challenge that can defeat you. No vision is insurmountable to the person who is filled with God-given courage.

3. Live in the faith zone, not the safe zone.

"Be strong and of good courage, and do it."

According to Nike company lore, one of the most famous and easily recognized slogans in advertising history was coined at a 1988 meeting of Nike's advertising agency, Wieden+Kennedy, and a group of Nike employees. Dan Wieden, speaking admiringly of Nike's can-do attitude, reportedly said, "You Nike guys—you just do it." The rest, as they say, is advertising history. Nike took on a new type of brand consciousness and broke advertising sound barriers with its unforgettable swoosh and phrase, *Just Do It.*

King David was the first to give those great words: "Solomon, just do it! Take the dream and do it. Make it happen. Perform the task." This is being in the faith zone, not the safe zone. This is the attitude possessed by every great dreamer in Scripture and every great dreamer of faith throughout history. Living in the safe zone robs us of our greatest moments and memories.

Just do it. Those simple little words are the secret to unleashing powerful results. The attitude of faith will move you to a crucial tipping point where you will go from *saying and planning* to *doing and proving!* Get rid of the *can't* words: *I can't. I don't have enough time. I don't have enough money. I don't know where to start.* Great dreamers start where they are and move into the future. Some examples from the Bible include:

- **Noah.** *"Noah did according to all that the LORD commanded him"* (Genesis 7:5).

- **Abraham.** *"It came to pass at that time that Abimelech and Phichol, the commander of his army, spoke to Abraham, saying, 'God is with you in all that you do'"* (Genesis 21:22).

- **David**. *"When He had removed him, He raised up for them David as king, to whom also He gave testimony and said, 'I have found David the son of Jesse, a man after My own heart, who will do all My will'"* (Acts 13:22).

Put your faith in God and His Word. Hear it. Obey it. Do it. Have faith in the God described in Numbers 23:19: *"God is not a man, that He should lie, nor a son of man, that He should repent. Has He said, and will He not do? Or has He spoken, and will He not make it good?"* Whatever it is, however hard it is, no matter what the cost is, no matter what the obstacles are, just shut your eyes, see the dream, and say, "I will do it!"

4. Reject intimidation and doubt relentlessly.

"Be strong and of good courage, and do it; do not fear nor be dismayed."

Fear of acting upon your dream will paralyze your life. Fear is a binding attitude that stops people from moving forward and shrinks dreams to human, "can-do" sizes. Fear prevents God-size dreams from being fulfilled. To dream big, God-size dreams, you must reject fear and intimidation with all your might.

Larry Page, the founder of Google, was interviewed about how to change the world, since his company has done just that. When asked how to get people to actually think about and work on things that might end up changing the world, he answered:

There are a number of barriers in place. Let me give an example. In our first founders' letter in 2004, we talked about the risk profile with respect to doing new innovations. We said we would do some things that would have only a 10% chance of making $1 billion over the long term. But we don't put many people on those things; 90% work on everything else. So that's not a big risk. And if you look at where many of our new features come from, it's from these riskier investments.

Even when we started Google, we thought, "Oh, we might fail," and we almost didn't do it. The reason we started is that Stanford said, "You guys can come back and finish your Ph.D.s if you don't succeed." Probably that one decision caused Google to be created. It's not clear we would have done it otherwise. We had all this internal risk we had just invented. It's not that we were going to starve or not get jobs or not have a good life or whatever, but you have this fear of failing and of doing something new, which is very natural. In order to do stuff that matters, you need to overcome that.[24]

To fulfill a God-size dream, you must reject fear and receive faith in huge doses. Fear is the emotional response to new challenges; it is the emotional response to the possibility of failure and the question, *What if...?* Here is God's response to fear:

- *"I will not be afraid"* (Psalm 3:6).
- *"I will fear no evil"* (Psalm 23:4).
- *"The LORD is on my side; I will not fear"* (Psalm 118:6).
- *"Fear not, for I am with you"* (Isaiah 41:10).
- *"Be not dismayed....I will help you"* (Isaiah 41:10).
- *"Fear not, for I have redeemed you"* (Isaiah 43:1).
- *"Fear not, for I am with you"* (Isaiah 43:5).
- *"Do not fear, for you will not be ashamed"* (Isaiah 54:4).
- *"Do not fear, let your hands be strong"* (Zechariah 8:13).

Fear not. Reject fear. Look fear in the face. Eleanor Roosevelt said,

You gain strength, courage, and confidence by every experience in which you really stop to look fear in the face....You must do the thing which you think you cannot do.[25]

Fear of failure is what almost stopped Larry Page from creating Google—a service that changed the world and the way people live today.

Fear of failure is closely related to fear of criticism or rejection. Successful faith dreamers overcome the fear of failure consistently, persistently, and daily. They look at mistakes as outcomes or results, not as failures. Those who stop dreaming look at mistakes as personal and permanent. Instead, learn through your failures and become stronger and wiser. Many people do not fulfill a fraction of their dreams because they are afraid to try and afraid to fail. Break out today. Just do it. Be bold. Take action. Change your circumstances by changing your attitude from fear to faith.

> *Change your circumstances by changing your attitude from fear to faith.*

5. Resist attitudes that beat you down.

"Do not fear nor be dismayed."

To *fear* is to be anxious or apprehensive about a possible or probable situation that is facing you. To be *dismayed* is to lose heart, to lose courage, to be disconcerted, and to be at a loss about how to deal with something. The Hebrew word used in 1 Chronicles 28:20 for *"dismayed"* is *chathath,* and it means "to be demoralized, broken, or beaten down."

Moving beyond fear to being dismayed is to be overcome by the obstacles that you face; it means losing heart and losing the ability to achieve the dream God has given you. When this happens, your faith becomes like a glass that has been thrown against the rocks and shattered into a million pieces. Do not allow the spirit of dismay to capture your life and blur your future.

When you begin to go after a God-size dream, you will face greater mountains to climb, greater obstacles to overcome, and greater chances of risk and failure. In the gospel of John, Jesus told us not to be dismayed. (See also Deuteronomy 1:21, 31:8; Joshua 1:9, 8:1; Psalm 143:4.)

> *Peace I leave with you: my own peace I give to you. It is not as the world gives its greetings that I give you peace. Let not your hearts be troubled or dismayed.* (John 14:27 WEY)

Nothing communicates what you feel and believe as much as the attitude of faith. You must throw off dismay and put on faith. The attitude of faith sees all things as possible. It believes that God is working for us and not against us.

6. Remember who your partner is: Yahweh.

"The LORD God; my God; will be with you. He will not leave you nor forsake you, until you have finished all the work."

In Old Testament times, a name was not only the identification but also the identity of the person. Many times, a special meaning was attached to the name. Names had, among other purposes, an explanatory purpose. Nabal's name meant "fool," and, in her explanation to David about his foolish action, his wife, Abigail, said, *"Nabal is his name, and folly is with him!"* (1 Samuel 25:25). Throughout Scripture, God revealed Himself to people through His names. The meanings behind God's names reveal the central personality and nature of the One who bears them.

Who is God to you? Who is the God of Scripture—the God revealed to us through Christ? Is He your most high God? Your all-sufficient God? Your Master, Lord of Peace, the Lord who will provide? To *hallow* a thing is to make it holy or to set it apart as something exalted and worthy of absolute devotion. To hallow the name of God is to regard Him with complete devotion and loving adoration. (See Nehemiah 9:5; Exodus 20:7; Leviticus 23:32.)

Your Partner for your dream is Jehovah, Yahweh, our God. Psalm 9:10 says, *"Those who know Your name will put their trust in You; for You, LORD, have not forsaken those who seek You."* We are in a partnership with the God whom Moses encountered—the God who first revealed His name to Moses.

> Then Moses said to God, *"Indeed, when I come to the children of Israel and say to them, 'The God of your fathers has sent me to you,' and they say to me, 'What is His name?' what shall I say to them?"* And God said to Moses, *"I AM WHO I AM."* And He said, *"Thus you shall say to the children of Israel, 'I AM has sent me to you.'"*   (Exodus 3:13–14)

In this passage, God's name is revealed as *Yahweh,* and in Hebrew, it is spelled without vowels: YHWH. YHWH is referred to as the holy *tetragrammaton,* which simply means the four letters. The modern English spelling is *Yahweh* or *Jehovah,* and it is the personal name of the God of Scripture. It is found 6,519 times in the Old Testament, and it signifies His redemptive, covenant-keeping promises to His redeemed people. The Greek equivalent is *Kurios*, meaning lord, master, or absolute ruler.

To Moses, this name became the passport for fulfilling the vision or dream that God had spoken to him. *Yahweh*—"I will be, or I am who I am, or I will be what I will be." The true meaning of *Yahweh* is, "I will show you who and what I am by who and what I will be to you, for I will be with you and I will be all that is necessary as the need arises."

This God is your Partner—the God who will be all that is necessary as needs arise in the pursuit and fulfillment of the God-size dream for your life. Daniel 11:32 says, *"Those who do wickedly against the covenant he shall corrupt with flattery; but the people who know their God shall be strong, and carry out great exploits."* The compound Jehovinistic names in Scripture reveal the sources that are available to those who know God.

- *Jehovah Jireh*—The Lord our Provider. (See Genesis 22:14; Philippians 4:19; Psalm 115:13.)

- *Jehovah Rapha*—The Lord our Healer. (See Exodus 15:26; Jeremiah 8:22; Psalm 6:2, 30:2, 103:3; Malachi 4:2.)

- *Jehovah Nissi*—The Lord our Banner. (See Exodus 17:15; Psalm 20:4; Deuteronomy 28:7; Isaiah 54:17; Isaiah 62:10.)

- *Jehovah Mekaddeshkem*—The Lord our Sanctification. (See Exodus 33:13; Leviticus 20:8; 1 Corinthians 6:11; 1 Thessalonians 5:23; 1 Corinthians 1:30.)

- *Jehovah Shalom*—The Lord our Peace. (See Judges 6:23–24; Numbers 6:24–26; Psalm 29:11, 35:27; Colossians 1:20–21.)

- *Jehovah Tsidkenu*—The Lord our Righteousness. (See Jeremiah 23:6, 33:16; Isaiah 48:10; Psalm 132:9; 2 Corinthians 5:21.)

- *Jehovah Shammah*—The Lord Is There. (See Ezekiel 48:35; Psalm 46:1–3, 11; Joshua 1:5; Hebrews 13:5.)

- *Jehovah Raah*—The Lord our Shepherd. (See Psalm 23:1, 28:9; Jeremiah 31:3; Lamentations 3:21–24.)

178 • The Attitude of Faith

We can pray in confidence, "Lord, I know You will be all that I need as the occasion arises. You are my Partner, and I will not limit You in any way."

Today is the day to extend your borders and fulfill your vision. God will not fail you, forsake you, or disappoint you. He is the true God who lives up to His name. He will not fail you, become slack, relax, abandon you, or desert you in a time of need. He promised Joshua, *"No man shall be able to stand before you all the days of your life; as I was with Moses, so I will be with you. I will not leave you nor forsake you"* (Joshua 1:5). That same promise is true for us today.

> *Faith is not merely you holding on to God but God holding on to you.*

Faith is not merely you holding on to God but God holding on to you. He will never let you go. Rely on the great God who is your Partner and reach for greatness. Keep moving forward until you have finished the entire dream and every last detail is completed. (See 1 Kings 6:9–14; Exodus 39:22, 40:33.) Make no small plans, for they have no capacity to stir heaven's full help and no capacity to stir other people's souls.

God is up to something that is so big and so unimaginably good that your mind cannot contain it. What we see God doing is never as good as what we cannot see Him doing.

Chapter 9

Yes to Healing

The attitude of faith for healing and miracles in our lives and in the lives of those around us is of absolute and vital importance. God has not changed. He *"is the same yesterday, today, and forever"* (Hebrews 13:8). The Holy Spirit is the same Holy Spirit who was in and upon Christ and the apostles, and He is upon us today. The same Holy Spirit who healed and worked miracles in the book of Acts is still working in the church today.

The last command of Christ, called the Great Commission, included healing the sick. (See Mark 16:17–18; Luke 13:11–13; Acts 28:8.) How is your faith for the supernatural release of healing in you, through you, and around you? We need more healing and miracles in our world today, and you are a key to connecting heaven and earth. Your willingness to pursue prayer for healing and miracles at any time in the life of every person with a need is critical. Believe, pray, and step out in faith. You are a person of faith.

We can see a rising interest in healing in contemporary society, but not all perspectives on healing come from a true understanding of God and His Word.

A Biblical Understanding of Healing

I believe that healing must be grounded in the reality of biblical theology. My approach to healing is based on the belief

> *Approach healing with the understanding that God is all-powerful and good and desires wholeness for all His people.*

that God is all-powerful and good. He desires healing and whole-ness for all His people.

Sickness Is Part of Our Fallen World

God created this world and all things in it, but the world we live in today is not the same world that God originally created. Sin entered the human race through Adam and Eve, the first transgres-sors. We live in a fallen world and are part of a fallen human race that is living out the consequences of sin and its judgment in our physical bodies. Yet we know that there will be a day when there will be no sin, no sickness, and no disease.

> *So when this corruptible has put on incorruption, and this mortal has put on immortality, then shall be brought to pass the saying that is written: "Death is swallowed up in victory."*
> (1 Corinthians 15:54)

However, we are still living in the age of sin, sickness, disease, and broken lives, and we have only a foretaste of the kingdom that is yet to come. The King lives in those who know Him as King, yet the kingdom in all its fullness and power is still to come.

Christ Brings Healing through Redemption

When we understand the problem in our universe, we must look immediately to Christ as our Savior and our Healer. Christ has made possible the healing we need in our hearts and our bodies through the redeeming act of His death, burial, and resurrection. This is what we call *redemption*. Redemption makes healing pos-sible. The healing we need is made available through the incarnate Son of God—through the power of the Holy Spirit in the context of the gospel of the new covenant, in which God restores wholeness to us by being our God.

God's healing power for us today is built upon the foundation of Christ our Redeemer. The English word for *redeemer* is derived from a Latin word meaning "to buy back," thus meaning the liberation of any possession, object, or person, usually by payment of a ransom.

The Greek word translated as *redeemer* means "to loose and to set free." The term refers to freeing from chains, slavery, or prison. In the theological context, the term *redemption* indicates a freeing from the slavery of sin or the ransom or price paid for freedom. F. F. Bruce, a well-known evangelical scholar, said of Jesus' miracles,

> While the miracles served as signs, they were not performed in order to be signs. They were as much a part and parcel of Jesus' ministry as was his preaching—not...seals affixed to the document to certify its genuineness but an integral element in the very text of the document.[26]

This is the gospel—the good news that Christ has come to give His life as a ransom for many. (See Matthew 10:28; Mark 10:45.) Our redemption is through the blood of Christ (see Ephesians 1:7), which includes forgiveness of sins (see Colossians 1:14) and healing for our bodies, souls, and spirits. Psalm 103:3–4 tells us about this God, *"Who forgives all your iniquities, Who heals all your diseases, Who redeems your life from destruction."* Christ has redeemed us from undesirable conditions in body, soul, and spirit, and He has made His healing power available to us.

We can be healed now, today, by the power of the cross, and we will be healed completely at the day of redemption—the second coming of Christ. (See Ephesians 4:30; Hebrews 9:12.) Jesus' healing ministry was integral to the gospel message that He preached. As New Testament scholar Alan Richardson states,

We can be healed now, today, by the power of the cross, and we will be healed completely at the day of redemption.

> The working of miracles is a part of the proclamation of the Kingdom of God, not an end in itself. Similarly, the sin of Chorazin and Bethsaida (Luke 10:13; Matthew 11:21) is spiritual blindness; they do not accept the preaching of the Kingdom of God or understand the miracles which were its inevitable concomitants.[27]

The message of the gospel cannot be separated from the miracle acts of the gospel.

Christ's redemptive work upon the cross is available to all who believe and extend their hearts toward Him in faith. The word *salvation* as used in the New Testament is the Greek word *sozo*. The word *sozo* means "to save, deliver, or protect," but it can also defined as "to heal, preserve, or make whole." The word *sozo* is translated in Matthew 9:21 as "to be made whole" and in Luke 8:36 as "healed": *"he who had been demon-possessed was healed."* In Acts 7:25, it is translated *"God would deliver them by his hand,"* and Acts 27:34 says, *"this is for your health"* (KJV).

In these different Scriptures, the word *sozo* is translated as "wholeness," "healing," "deliverance," and "health." Salvation is to be understood in its full work of not only healing the soul from sin but also making God's power available to heal the body from sickness. According to Dutch New Testament scholar H. Van der Loos,

> The miracles were therefore not works or signs which happened for the sake of the apostles, but originated in the point at issue, viz. the proclamation of salvation by Jesus Christ and the coming of His kingdom. They did not accompany the preaching of the gospels as incidentals, but formed an integral part of it; in the healing, as a visible function of the Kingdom of God, something that could be experienced, God's will to heal the whole of man was manifested.[28]

Christ was not only the Messiah who would save us from sin but also the Messiah who would heal us from sickness.

The Scriptures present Christ as both Savior and Healer. Isaiah 53:5 states that *"by His stripes we are healed,"* and Matthew 8:16–17 tells us that Jesus *"healed all who were sick, that it might be fulfilled which was spoken by Isaiah the prophet, saying: 'He Himself took our infirmities and bore our sicknesses.'"* The New Testament establishes and confirms the Old Testament by showing that Christ was not only the Messiah who would save us from sin but also the Messiah who would heal us from sickness.

As mentioned in the last chapter, one of the Old Testament compound names for Jehovah is *Jehovah Rapha*, "the Lord our Healer." Jesus not only takes our sin; he also takes our sicknesses. The word *rapha* in Hebrew means "restoring to normal." Matthew 9:35 says that Christ came *"preaching the gospel of the kingdom, and healing every sickness and every disease,"* a concept repeated in Matthew 10:1: *"He gave them power...to heal all manner of sickness and all manner of disease"* (KJV). In *The City of God*, Saint Augustine declared,

> Once I realized how many miracles were occurring in our own day and which were so like the miracles of old and also how wrong it would be to allow the memory of these marvels of divine power to perish from among our people. It is only two years ago that the keeping of records was begun here in Hippo. And already, at this writing, we have nearly seventy attested miracles.[29]

Christ's Redemptive Healing Is for All Our Diseases

Man is born into sin; therefore, he is born with a disease—not just a disease of the body, but *a disease of the understanding, the will, the affections, and the mind.*

Christ came to heal us from a disease of the **understanding**. (See 1 Corinthians 2:11–15.) Our natural understanding is totally incapable of comprehending spiritual things. We need healing—healing of the understanding. Our understanding is corrupted by sin. The Holy Spirit will allow light, life, and healing to come into your understanding so that you can see and understand the secret things of God.

> *These things we also speak, not in words which man's wisdom teaches but which the Holy Spirit teaches, comparing spiritual things with spiritual. But the natural man does not receive the things of the Spirit of God, for they are foolishness to him; nor can he know them, because they are spiritually discerned.*
> (1 Corinthians 2:13–14)

Jesus also came to heal the disease of the **will**. *"All we like sheep have gone astray; we have turned, every one, to his own way"* (Isaiah 53:6).

Our wills are naturally stubborn. We are inclined to turn to that which is opposed to God. Through the blood of Christ and through the power of the Holy Spirit, our wills can be healed, and we can become truly obedient to the Holy Spirit.

Christ's redemption can also heal the disease of our **affections**. *"Set your mind on things above, not on things on the earth. For you died, and your life is hidden with Christ in God"* (Colossians 3:2–3). The affections of the heart can be alienated, but God, through the Holy Spirit, communicates an impulse to the soul whereby the poisonous influences are destroyed and our affections are restored to God.

Christ's redemption can also heal the diseases of our **minds**. *"For to be carnally minded is death, but to be spiritually minded is life and peace"* (Romans 8:6). The mind under the influence of the fallen world can be bent, perverted, and bombarded until it is sick. Our minds need the healing of God, which is brought by the power of the Holy Spirit. Christ's redemption heals any and all diseases that touch our bodies. (See Romans 8:23.) Justin Martyr said,

> For numberless demoniacs throughout the whole world, and in your city [Rome], many of our Christian men exorcising them in the Name of Jesus Christ…have healed and do heal, rendering helpless and driving the possessing devils out of the men, though they could not be cured by all the other exorcists, and those who used incantations and drugs.[30]

Healing Is for Today

It is right to believe for the full restoration of the church's gifts, as seen in the book of Acts, with a full manifestation of God's power in signs, wonders, and healings. It is right to fast and pray, believing God for more Holy Spirit power and authority in order to see more miracles in today's world. We must pray for miracles and healings, believing the sick will improve or be healed completely.

In times past, the church has suffered from faulty theology concerning healing and miracles. Generally speaking, the church bought into the theology that the age of miracles had ceased with the apostolic period of the church, and that God no longer healed people as He had then. This view is limited and erroneous. The church of today seems to have descended to the level of the natural in preaching, soulwinning, doing church, and ministering healing. The gifts of the Spirit have been supplanted by the arts of logic and rhetoric.

God desires the miraculous to function today, now, in the church. He desires for the gifts to be operating fully with a full release of supernatural power through believing Christians. We must promote a biblical interest in God's people to pursue genuine, authentic, supernatural healings and miracles in the twenty-first century.

> *God desires the miraculous to function today, now, in the church.*

Today, there are some extreme practices within Pentecostal groups, which have caused reactions, questions, and even a denial of the healing ministry. Nevertheless, we must lift the healing ministry to a level of unquestionable integrity and develop a healthy respect for the power of God as demonstrated through miracles. Healing and gift-based ministry are simply normal and biblical parts of the healthy church and the healthy believer's life. Healing prayer is part of the normal Christian life. It should not be elevated in the community of faith, nor should it be undervalued. It must simply be kept in balance.

Personal Testimony

Peter

Becoming a firefighter is very difficult in my city. After six months of tests and interviews, I was chosen to be one of forty people hired out of three thousand applicants. I found myself excitedly facing a new career and future. The last stage of the hiring process was spending three hours with a doctor as he checked everything you could think of about the body. What did I have to worry about? I had the fastest time in physical tryouts and endurance testing, I was twenty-six, and I was in great shape. All I had to do was show up.

The very last stage of my physical testing was a stress test. At the end, looking concerned, the doctor informed me that he could not recommend I be hired because of an abnormal heartbeat. I had to go see a cardiovascular specialist for further tests. This was not what I wanted to hear because I had no insurance and could visualize the bills piling up. The career of a lifetime was fading from sight.

I first had to go to a doctor who could give me a referral to a cardiologist. He had me bring my test results and began to look through them. After about twenty minutes of examining the reams of paper that showed my heartbeat from the tests, he told me that the heartbeat on the paper was that of a sixty-five-year-old man with heart disease. He then told me we needed to pray, so we knelt together and prayed. The second doctor I went to reviewed the previous test and agreed that I had a sixty-five-year-old heart and would be needing heart surgery within the next few months. He gave me a list of the three best doctors he would go to if he were in my shoes, so I made an appointment with one of them.

When I met with the specialist, he did an echocardiogram and, after examining the results, said that my heartbeat from the first test did not match the second one. I had a normal, healthy, strong heart.

What happened between those two tests? God.

God Uses Different Methods to Heal

People may be healed in a variety of ways. There are healing miracles that are miracles of creation. The healing of the man born without eyesight who received perfect eyes is a creative miracle that required God's creative power. (See John 9:1–12.) There are also instantaneous miracles and healings. We see this in the miracle of the man at the Pool of Bethesda, who was instantly given full healing. (See John 5:1–15.)

There are also miracles that intervene in the operation of natural processes. These miracles of healing occur when God brings about healing through doctors, medicine, and hospitals. God can work providentially within the natural order over a period of time to bring about healing, working within the framework of His own natural laws.

There are also miracles of healing that take place slowly, not instantaneously, but are outside of the natural laws. The creative power of God is at work, healing the sickness. The sickness is not treated by medicine, but the person continues to get better, receiving healing by prayer and faith. It is a slow recovery and a work of healing, but it is supernatural.

At our church, we pray for healing all the time, and we see answers come in many different ways. One young woman was diagnosed with ovarian cancer when she was only thirty years old. After surgery and chemotherapy, the cancer left, and she is still cancer-free more than seventeen years later. Another woman had suffered from stomach problems for years. She was prayed for during a church service, and the next morning, as she reached for her medication, she felt a prompting from the Holy Spirit and set the medicine back in the cabinet. She went back to the doctor, asked him to run the tests again, and discovered that her ulcer and hernia were gone—without medical intervention.

Commit to Pray for Healing

We can continually improve our prayers for healing. We must make a commitment to move out of head-knowledge and into faith-habit. We must pray for the sick every time we have a chance. We have to move from intellectual knowledge to observational knowledge to experiential knowledge. We not only have a belief system for healings and miracles, but we also have a faith attitude—faith that something can and will happen.

> *We must make a commitment to move out of head-knowledge and into faith-habit.*

Prayer for healing is often a process that requires time, faith, and patience. We may pray over the same person as many times as it takes. We can pray for the pain to stop. If the pain stops, it does not necessarily mean that the healing is complete. It can be the beginning of a healing or a sign that the healing has begun. We can pray for the medical treatments to bring healing without harmful side effects. We can pray for protection. We can pray for the medicine to be expanded and work beyond its normal power. We can pray for the sickness or disease to stop in its tracks and go no further.

It is right to be a channel of divine power into other people's lives at their points of need. Paul said, *"We have this treasure in earthen vessels, that the excellence of the power may be of God and not of us"* (2 Corinthians 4:7). This verse encourages me to believe that I am empowered to do more than I think I can do because of the treasure that God has put in me. I must not let the lack of good experiences rule out what God seeks to do in my life and in the lives of others. I have authority. (See Luke 9:1.) I have anointing. (See 2 Corinthians 1:21.) I have faith. (See 2 Corinthians 4:13.) I believe that God does not lie. (See Numbers 23:19.) I have all the power I need. (See Mark 9:18.)

Personal Testimony

Randy

I became a Christian at forty-two, and my pastor encouraged me to read the Bible in one year. I told him I couldn't do it because I was dyslexic and had never read a book cover to cover before in my life. I had read newspaper articles or short stories in *Reader's Digest*, but never a book. He told me, "You can do all things through Christ who strengthens you." (See Philippians 4:13.) Then, he encouraged me to sit down every day and pray, asking God to help me and renew my mind; then, I should try to read a passage of Scripture.

One year later, I finished the Bible. I read it cover to cover, and when I was finished, my mind had been renewed, and I was cured of dyslexia. Since then, I have gone to college and earned a bachelor's degree in theology.

Believe for Healings Today

Christ has not taken back His power. Healings have not ceased. Christ has not changed. He still delivers. He still heals. *"Jesus Christ is the same yesterday, today, and forever"* (Hebrews 13:8). I have settled in my heart that I will contend for the supernatural to be present in my life, my ministry, my church, and my world.

In Mark 9:23, Jesus said, *"If you can believe, all things are possible to him who believes."* Our commitment must be to build a strong atmosphere of expectation through sound, biblical faith for healings and miracles. There has been and still seems to be a suppressed attitude toward expectation. It may be that people are afraid to expect miracles from God because there has been much disappointment in this area.

The biblical heritage is a belief in the power of the Holy Spirit to do great and mighty things. There are many types of churches that believe in miracles and healings, and they represent a variety of methodologies. Our roots must be biblical, but our methodology can be contemporary and creative when it comes to the ministry of healing and miracles. Healing is an avenue to manifest the compassion of Christ (see Matthew 14:14), to prove Christ's authenticity (see John 5:36), and to destroy the works of the devil (see 1 John 3:8).

The healing ministry is an extension of the power of the kingdom of God on earth now, and it is a ministry that needs to be carried out by all who know Christ and have the Holy Spirit. You could have trained prayer teams that pray for anyone desiring prayer for healing. During the worship service, they could wait in a designated location for those who desire prayer and minister to the needs of the people for as long as it takes. Healing teams could also minister at the end of the service as the pastoral team anoints with oil and lays hands on those requesting healing prayer, according to James 5:14.

> *The healing ministry is an extension of the power of the kingdom of God on earth.*

Believe in the God Who Heals

If you diligently heed the voice of the LORD your God and do what is right in His sight, give ear to His commandments and keep all His statutes, I will put none of the diseases on you which I have brought on the Egyptians. For I am the LORD who heals you.
(Exodus 15:26)

Now see that I, even I, am He, and there is no God besides Me; I kill and I make alive; I wound and I heal; nor is there any who can deliver from My hand. (Deuteronomy 32:39)

"For I will restore health to you and heal you of your wounds," says the LORD, "Because they called you an outcast saying: 'This is Zion; no one seeks her.'" (Jeremiah 30:17)

Behold, I will bring it health and healing; I will heal them and reveal to them the abundance of peace and truth.
(Jeremiah 33:6)

Come, and let us return to the LORD; for He has torn, but He will heal us; He has stricken, but He will bind us up. (Hosea 6:1)

Then your light shall break forth like the morning, your healing shall spring forth speedily, and your righteousness shall go before you; the glory of the LORD shall be your rear guard.
(Isaiah 58:8)

But to you who fear My name the Sun of Righteousness shall arise with healing in His wings; and you shall go out and grow fat like stall-fed calves. (Malachi 4:2)

In the middle of its street, and on either side of the river, was the tree of life, which bore twelve fruits, each tree yielding its fruit every month. The leaves of the tree were for the healing of the nations.
(Revelation 22:2)

He sent His word and healed them, and delivered them from their destructions. (Psalm 107:20)

He was wounded for our transgressions, He was bruised for our iniquities; the chastisement for our peace was upon Him, and by His stripes we are healed. (Isaiah 53:5)

And it shall be that every living thing that moves, wherever the rivers go, will live. There will be a very great multitude of fish, because these waters go there; for they will be healed, and everything will live wherever the river goes. (Ezekiel 47:9)

I Believe in Jesus Who Heals

"The Spirit of the LORD is upon Me, because He has anointed Me to preach the gospel to the poor; He has sent Me to heal the brokenhearted, to proclaim liberty to the captives and recovery of sight to the blind, to set at liberty those who are oppressed...." When the sun was setting, all those who had any that were sick with various diseases brought them to Him; and He laid His hands on every one of them and healed them. (Luke 4:18, 40)

He said to them, "You will surely say this proverb to Me, 'Physician, heal yourself! Whatever we have heard done in Capernaum, do also here in Your country.'" (Luke 4:23)

God anointed Jesus of Nazareth with the Holy Spirit and with power, who went about doing good and healing all who were oppressed by the devil, for God was with Him. (Acts 10:38)

There was a man who had a withered hand. And they asked Him, saying, "Is it lawful to heal on the Sabbath?"; that they might accuse Him....But when Jesus knew it, He withdrew from there. And great multitudes followed Him, and He healed them all. (Matthew 12:10, 15)

Now it happened on a certain day, as He was teaching, that there were Pharisees and teachers of the law sitting by, who had come out of every town of Galilee, Judea, and Jerusalem. And the power of the Lord was present to heal them. Then behold, men brought on a bed a man who was paralyzed, whom they sought to bring in and lay before Him. (Luke 5:17–18)

Jesus went about all Galilee, teaching in their synagogues, preaching the gospel of the kingdom, and healing all kinds of sickness and all kinds of disease among the people. Then His fame went throughout all Syria; and they brought to Him all sick people who were afflicted with various diseases and torments, and those who were demon-possessed, epileptics, and paralytics; and He healed them. (Matthew 4:23–24)

A woman of Canaan came from that region and cried out to Him, saying, "Have mercy on me, O Lord, Son of David! My daughter is severely demon-possessed."...Jesus answered and said to her, "O woman, great is your faith! Let it be to you as you desire." And her daughter was healed from that very hour....Then great multitudes came to Him, having with them the lame, blind, mute, maimed, and many others; and they laid them down at Jesus' feet, and He healed them. (Matthew 15:22, 28, 30)

Then the blind and the lame came to Him in the temple, and He healed them. (Matthew 21:14)

I Believe We Have Received Christ's Ministry of Healing

When He had called His twelve disciples to Him, He gave them power over unclean spirits, to cast them out, and to heal all kinds of sickness and all kinds of disease....Heal the sick, cleanse the lepers, raise the dead, cast out demons. Freely you have received, freely give. (Matthew 10:1, 8)

[Jesus appointed them] *to have power to heal sicknesses and to cast out demons.* (Mark 3:15)

He sent them to preach the kingdom of God and to heal the sick. (Luke 9:2)

Heal the sick there, and say to them, "The kingdom of God has come near to you." (Luke 10:9)

As the lame man who was healed held on to Peter and John, all the people ran together to them in the porch which is called Solomon's, greatly amazed. So when Peter saw it, he responded to the people: "Men of Israel, why do you marvel at this? Or why look so intently at us, as though by our own power or godliness we had made this man walk?" (Acts 3:11–12)

Seeing the man who had been healed standing with them, they could say nothing against it. (Acts 4:14)

A multitude gathered from the surrounding cities to Jerusalem, bringing sick people and those who were tormented by unclean spirits, and they were all healed. (Acts 5:16)

Unclean spirits, crying with a loud voice, came out of many who were possessed; and many who were paralyzed and lame were healed. (Acts 8:7)

This man heard Paul speaking. Paul, observing him intently and seeing that he had faith to be healed.... (Acts 14:9)

The father of Publius lay sick of a fever and dysentery. Paul went in to him and prayed, and he laid his hands on him and healed him. (Acts 28:8)

Is anyone among you sick? Let him call for the elders of the church, and let them pray over him, anointing him with oil in the name of the Lord. And the prayer of faith will save the sick, and the Lord will raise him up. And if he has committed sins, he will be forgiven. (James 5:14–15)

> **The Source of all healing is God, but the avenues God uses for healing can be many.**

The Source of all healing is God, but the avenues God uses for healing can be many. Healing is the very heart of who God is. The Scriptures tell us repeatedly that God is all-powerful and all-loving. These words remain platitudes and God remains an abstraction until they are applied in real situations. Believe that healing is in Christ and is for today. Believe that it is an important part of the gospel message.

God can use skill and science, doctors, nutritionists, trainers, and counselors to promote healing. God can use partaking of the Lord's Table in Communion as a point of faith for physical, emotional, and spiritual healing. God can use people who have gifts of healing and faith for miracles to bring healing to others. God can use praying believers who agree together in prayer to bring healing.

God can use all methods, but most important, God can use *you*. Let your faith attitude for healing grow, and grow, and grow. Do not get discouraged and give up on praying for God to heal.

Chapter 10

Yes to the Attitude of Faith

Two young girls peeked through the kitchen door to find Grandpa taking his afternoon nap on the couch. Their idea seemed quite safe: get some Limburger cheese from the fridge and put it on Grandpa's mustache while he was sleeping. The idea moved to reality as they found the cheese, quietly applied it to Grandpa's mustache, and then snuck back up the stirs to watch what would happen.

Grandpa awakened quickly with a big stretch and a funny look on his face. "What smells so horrible in here?" He called his wife into the family room to let her know that she should clean the room because it had a horrible smell. She couldn't smell anything, so she shrugged him off as only a grandma can shrug off an irritable grandpa.

He went into the kitchen to make himself a cup of tea. The kitchen smelled awful, too, so he called his wife and told her the kitchen was the source of the odor, and she needed to clean it first. Unable to handle the horrific smell in his house, he went outside to escape. But as he relaxed on the front porch, the smell was just as strong there as inside. Grumbling, Grandpa concluded, "The whole world stinks!"

When you have a bad attitude, it follows you like Limburger cheese under your nose. Everywhere you go, it is there. You will blame your friends, your job, your boss, your family, the economy, the environment, anything and everything. They all smell bad to you because the problem is right under your nose—it is your own bad attitude.

Attitude Is Everything

Attitude is the shaping influence of your life, and you can create it, change it, revise it, align it, improve it, and make it either a helper or a hindrance to your life. You must develop a healthy, biblical, positive, faith-filled attitude. It is not automatic. It takes work. But wrong attitudes can block the favor and blessings that God desires to give you. Attitudes erode if not protected and improved consistently and persistently. Your attitude may well be the most important and valuable thing you have in your possession right now.

Your attitude may well be the most important and valuable thing you have in your possession right now.

Airplanes have what is called an *attitude indicator*, which is one of the most important pieces of equipment pilots rely upon. It is placed in the most prominent position on the instrument panel so it is always in front of the pilot's gaze. This instrument indicates the position of the aircraft in relation to the horizon. The attitude of the airplane affects its performance, and the attitude must change in order to change performance.

So it is with life. Our attitudes are indications of where our lives are headed. Attitude can mean the difference between fulfilling your God-given dreams and letting them die. Attitude can be what motivates a boss to promote or demote an employee. The most significant decision you can make on a daily basis is your choice of the attitude that will shape your life. For some, attitude presents a difficulty in every opportunity. For others, it permits an opportunity in every difficulty.

When your attitude is biblical, God anchored, Holy Spirit empowered, and Word of God driven, there is no barrier too high, no valley too deep, and no dream too big or too extreme. In the *Amplified Bible*, Philippians 2:5 says, *"Let this same attitude and purpose and [humble] mind be in you which was in Christ Jesus [Let Him be your example in humility]."* Attitude is a settled mode of thinking—including beliefs, convictions, and opinions about a person, subject, or action—that determines behavior.

The attitude I want to deal with is the attitude of faith—the attitude that gives us an uncommonly positive perspective on all aspects of life. Nothing can stop you from achieving God's best for your life and the lives you touch of other people in the journey when the attitude of faith is working in you. The attitude of faith opens and closes doors, makes a way where there is no way, and sees things that others cannot see.

Since we have the same spirit of faith, according to what is written, "I believed and therefore I spoke," we also believe and therefore speak. (2 Corinthians 4:13)

We believe, and therefore, we speak out words of faith for our futures, our potentials, our visions, and our dreams. We have the attitude that says, "Yes, God is awesome. Yes, God loves me and desires to do great things in my life." The attitude of faith sees God as the God who is not limited—a great God who loves to help us do the impossible.

Like the apostles, pray Luke 17:5: "*The apostles said to the Lord, 'Increase our faith.'*" "Increase my faith, Jesus. Increase my capacity to believe and rise to the challenges that I face. Increase my faith for resources, for open doors, and for the favor of God to rain upon my life." Respond like the blind men in Matthew 9:28:

When He had come into the house, the blind men came to Him. And Jesus said to them, "Do you believe that I am able to do this?" They said to Him, "Yes, Lord."

The response of the attitude of faith is always, "Yes, Lord." The attitude of faith sees that God is great. "*Looking for the blessed hope and glorious appearing of our great God and Savior Jesus Christ...*" (Titus 2:13). "*Great*" means notable, remarkable, and extraordinary in power. That is our God. Deuteronomy 10:17 says, "*The LORD your God is God of gods and Lord of lords, the great God, mighty and awesome, who shows no partiality nor takes a bribe.*" We sing the song of the greatness of our God with all those who have believed in Him.

They sing the song of Moses, the servant of God, and the song of the Lamb, saying: "Great and marvelous are Your works, Lord God Almighty! Just and true are Your ways, O King of the saints!" (Revelation 15:3)

Take time right now to read and meditate on some of these great faith Scriptures as you cultivate an attitude of great faith in a great God.

Now to Him who is able to do exceedingly abundantly above all that we ask or think, according to the power that works in us....
(Ephesians 3:20)

When Jesus heard these things, He marveled at him, and turned around and said to the crowd that followed Him, "I say to you, I have not found such great faith, not even in Israel!"
(Luke 7:9)

Without faith it is impossible to please Him, for he who comes to God must believe that He is, and that He is a rewarder of those who diligently seek Him.
(Hebrews 11:6)

So then faith comes by hearing, and hearing by the word of God.
(Romans 10:17)

> *Great faith sees the invisible, believes the incredible, and receives the impossible.*

Great faith sees the invisible, believes the incredible, and receives the impossible. Great faith sees all the promised blessings as if they were present possessions. The attitude of faith believes that God is a good God, a God of abundance, and an all-things-are-possible God. It believes that God is all-powerful at all times and in every circumstance—that He is a God who is able to do anything.

Faith is the empty hand of the soul that reaches out to God and comes back full! Faith in your hand reaches up to receive what God has freely promised. If the devil can pull your hand back down to your side, then he has succeeded. So reach. Reach high. Reach right now with your hand and simply say, "God, I am a person of great faith, and I am reaching out to You with the attitude of faith to receive all that You have for my life."

Trust God's Promises for the Future

Faith is not just about the present. It is not about the things you can capture right now with a camera. Rather, it is about the things in the future that God has promised. Faith is the ability of the human spirit that is filled with the Holy Spirit to open up and receive impressions from God that are born from His Word and made alive by His Spirit. This ability brings about a supernatural conviction of certain facts, apart from the senses.

God is challenging you to live with the attitude of faith. The great vision for your life will demand great faith—a faith that reaches forward, a faith that stretches into the new. Faith lives on challenge. Faith rises to meet the enemies of your life. Faith never stands still, but it moves out of the boat—and out of the box—to possess. It does not take no as the answer to big challenges. Faith always finds a way to say, "Yes, Lord. I believe all things are possible with You. Yes, Lord. I am willing to risk, step out, and step over. I am willing to be tested."

When faced with great challenges that restrict or limit our dreams, we must break out in faith or be doomed to living in the closet instead of in the whole house that God has for us. My life is driven by this faith attitude spirit and principle. Without this attitude, I would have settled for less, missed the high calling, and lived at a lower level than what God desired for me. I have grasped the importance of the attitude of faith, and it has become my most valuable possession.

When faced with great challenges that restrict or limit our dreams, we must break out in faith.

Recently, our church faced a pivotal decision. The eight of us on the core executive leadership team were discussing our campus situation and how we were landlocked with insufficient parking space to grow. We did not have the most accessible location, and we would have to make several big changes in order to position ourselves to better minister to our city.

Then, the strangest thing came out of my mouth. I simply said, "We can stay where we are and enjoy our beautiful thirty-three-acre property with our K–12 school, four-year Bible College, publishing company, and three-thousand-seat sanctuary and let the next generation of leaders deal with this massive challenge looming in front of us. If we don't have the grace, the strength, and the faith to rise to this challenge, we can wait a few more years and let a younger group of leaders climb this mountain."

I asked the leaders to give me their feelings on this faith challenge, which would require a massive amount of future work, new resources, and multiplie millions of dollars. Each leader responded with a deep sense that God was in the room and that we were determining our future and the futures of all who followed us. We could stay, be satisfied, enjoy, and use what we already had, appreciating the level of success and fulfillment that was already ours, or we could get out of the boat, break out of the box, and launch an aggressive new vision, taking the risk to go for the gold.

Each leader made a crossover decision and said, "Yes, we will rise to the challenge. We will not be limited by these factors. Like Caleb, we are more than able to go up and take this mountain." It was one of those moments that made me very proud to serve with leaders who had the attitude of faith and were willing to be stretched once again. That day opened up a whole new realm of faith, vision, and resources that we could have passed by if we had not entered the door of faith.

We moved into our future with a brand-new, multisite church campus vision that opened up the whole metro area to our vision and has now become a way of life for us. We went from two weekend services to our current eleven weekend services and four weekday services for a total of fifteen services a week! The attitude of faith put us into a realm of doing life and ministry that was not present until after we said, "Yes, Lord. We are willing. Get us out of the boat and take us to another level."

The Scripture that helped me on this faith journey will also help you cultivate the attitude of faith:

> *Then the children of Joseph spoke to Joshua, saying, "Why have you given us only one lot and one share to inherit, since we are a great people, inasmuch as the LORD has blessed us until now?" So Joshua answered them, "If you are a great people, then go up to the forest country and clear a place for yourself there in the land of the Perizzites and the giants, since the mountains of Ephraim are too confined for you." But the children of Joseph said, "The mountain country is not enough for us; and all the Canaanites who dwell in the land of the valley have chariots of*

iron, both those who are of Beth Shean and its towns and those who are of the Valley of Jezreel." And Joshua spoke to the house of Joseph; to Ephraim and Manasseh; saying, "You are a great people and have great power; you shall not have only one lot, but the mountain country shall be yours. Although it is wooded, you shall cut it down, and its farthest extent shall be yours; for you shall drive out the Canaanites, though they have iron chariots and are strong." (Joshua 17:14–18)

These Scriptures discuss Ephraim and Manasseh, who came to Joshua and said, "We are limited and restricted. We do not have enough room to grow, and we want more." Ephraim and Manasseh were children of Joseph, so they had in their bloodstreams the attitude of faith for dreams and visions. Joseph was a dreamer. His name meant "to add or increase," and that was his life. God added to him what others did not have: a God-dream, a mantle given by his father, and a long, hard road to see the fulfillment of his dream.

Ephraim and Manasseh had this same spirit and would not be limited by any boundaries that man had put up. They wanted increase, more vision, and more room. They said to Joshua, "We are a great people, and we deserve more room. We do not want just one share for our inheritance." They were not a one-lot people. They could see that there was more than one lot of land available. The mountain country was not enough for them. They were confined, restricted, restrained, curbed, and cramped. It was too small!

If you can identify with Ephraim and Manasseh in feeling this confinement, then you are in a great place to be enlarged forever. This is the place to say, "Yes, Lord. I believe. I will not be confined." Do not shrink to the size of your current position. It is often said that if a shark is put in a small container, it will grow only as large as the size of that tank. Do not shrink the size of your fish tank and limit your ability to grow. Hudson Taylor, the great faith missionary to China, said, "Satan may build a hedge about us and fence us in and hinder our movements, but he cannot roof us in and prevent our looking up."[31]

Do not shrink to the size of your current position.

Joshua's reply to Ephraim and Manasseh in Joshua 17:17 represented the words of God—words that would break them out of their constraint: *"You are a great people and have great power; you shall not have only one lot."* Joshua was saying, "If you are a great people, so be it. But if you are a great people, you must be capable of great faith deeds. Get on with it. There are great opportunities before you, wooded mountain areas that no one has cleared before because the work is hard and dangerous. There are great rewards lying within reach, but you must direct your energies toward them. They are waiting for someone who will do the work required. There are enemies who possess your lot of inheritance, so go up, fight them, and take what is yours."

There is no room for blaming God for your lot in life, your one talent, your limited resources, or your limited opportunities. You are not to sit back and complain about what has been dealt to you, but you are to rise to the challenge and change your circumstances with the attitude of faith, vision, and hard work.

A story is told that in ancient times, a king placed a boulder in the middle of the road and then hid nearby to see if anyone would remove it. Some of the king's wealthiest courtiers and merchants simply walked around it. Many loudly blamed the king for not keeping the roads clear, but none did anything about getting the big stone out of the way. Then, a peasant came along carrying a load of vegetables. On approaching the boulder, the peasant laid down his burden and tried to move the stone to the side of the road.

After much pushing and straining, the peasant finally succeeded. As he picked up his load of vegetables, he noticed a purse lying in the road where the boulder had been. The purse contained many gold coins and a note from the king indicating that the gold was for the person who removed the boulder from the roadway. The peasant learned what many others never understand: that every obstacle presents an opportunity to improve one's condition.

There is another story of a ten-year-old girl who had been born with a crippled leg and had to wear a brace. She came home from school one day, talking excitedly about her day. The students had competed in races that day, and she had won two of them, even with her crippled leg and brace. Her father was surprised and secretly wondered how she could have accomplished that. She confirmed his suspicions when she said, "I had an advantage." *Of course*, her father thought. *They gave her a head start because of her handicap.* But before he could say anything, she exclaimed, "Daddy, I didn't get a head start. My advantage was that I had to try harder!"

Perhaps the deck seems stacked against you and the challenges you face seem too great to overcome. But you have the advantage of great faith. You can rise to the challenge, work harder, overcome the obstacle, and see a great reward. Do not look for the easy races, the easy challenges, or the easy inheritance. Dream big, ask largely, and believe for great things.

> *Dream big, ask largely, and believe for great things.*

The name *Disney* is known worldwide today, but that is because Walt Disney dreamed big. He would not settle for the small dreams that anyone could accomplish. He reached for the big ones that no one believed were possible. When he went to his board with a plan, he would lay out a dream that was massive and overwhelming and then sit back to see the board members' responses. If they stared at him in disbelief and shock and then resisted the idea, he pursued it. If they simply accepted it with no argument, he dropped it.

He refused to pursue a dream so small that anyone could believe it. Only dreams big enough to challenge everyone who heard them were dreams big enough to pursue!

Personal Testimony

Ralph

When we moved to Portland in early 2001, the Northwest was experiencing one of the most challenging economic downturns in decades. Words like *recession, shortages, cutbacks*, and *unemployment* dominated the daily headlines. Having spent much of my professional life as an IT recruiter, I was deeply concerned about two things: the tens of thousands of jobless Oregonians left in the wake of a 9 percent rate of unemployment, and the huge need for an online job advertiser for our local companies.

This concern compelled my wife and me to give ourselves to an extended season of prayer and fasting. We wanted to do something to help unemployed families. It was during this season of prayer that an idea for a new business began to develop.

We knew that any business startup would have its share of difficulties, so our first step was to get confirmation that God was not only receptive to the idea but also its originator. So, in addition to continued prayer, we sought counsel from seasoned business owners and professionals in our church family. We also obtained the services of a market research company to explore the business community's receptivity to our idea. Every indicator seemed to be a green light.

The next few months were nothing short of grueling—physically, emotionally, financially, and spiritually. And while we had developed a business plan carefully and mapped out a development budget and timeline, reality often proved to be more difficult than our best-laid plans. The eighteen-hour days and shrinking bank account were taking their toll. More than once, it was the prayers and support of my wife and a committed group of business friends at church, and the assurance that God was with us, that sustained us through those trying days.

Today, that startup company is the Northwest's leading job advertising site. It has been not only a great blessing to our family and the families of those who work with us, but it has also helped secure jobs for literally tens of thousands of Northwest job seekers and helped thousands of local companies advertise available jobs. And that was our dream all along.

Joshua's Challenge to Ephraim and Manasseh

Go Up

Joshua challenged Ephraim and Manasseh to act on their faith and go up, not allowing themselves to be confined.

If you are a great people, then go up to the forest country and clear a place for yourself there in the land of the Perizzites and the giants, since the mountains of Ephraim are too confined for you. (Joshua 17:15, emphasis added)

Go up. Do not stay within your set boundaries. Do not blame your circumstances. Move out. Get up and go forward. See the vision that God has set before you and then make a pivotal attitude adjustment from "I can't" to "I can" to "I will."

This is the attitude seen when God challenged Jacob to go up. *"Arise, go up to Bethel and dwell there; and make an altar there to God, who appeared to you when you fled from the face of Esau your brother"* (Genesis 35:1). He was to arise and go up to meet God, and there he was to build an altar of prayer and dedication. God told Moses, *"Go, and I will be with your mouth and teach you what you shall say"* (Exodus 4:12).

Caleb had this faith attitude. While the rest of the children of Israel were quaking in fear and refusing to lay hold of the promise of God, Caleb spoke up and said, *"Let us go up at once and take possession, for we are well able to overcome it"* (Numbers 13:30). He did not think they could barely overcome the giants or that there was a slim possibility they could take the land. He said, "We are well able. We have everything we need in God to take possession of our promised inheritance." The basis of his faith was the same as Joshua's.

Have I not commanded you? Be strong and of good courage; do not be afraid, nor be dismayed, for the LORD your God is with you wherever you go. (Joshua 1:9)

The word for you is *go up*. Rise up. Believe. Meet your God. You are well able in Him. He will be with you. Move into the realm of faith, and God will do what you cannot.

> *Move into the realm of faith, and God will do what you cannot.*

Cut Down

The attitude of faith moves us to *go up* to our mountain country. Go up to the place of challenges and hard work described by Joshua.

The mountain country shall be yours. Although it is wooded, you shall cut it down, and its farthest extent shall be yours; for you shall drive out the Canaanites, though they have iron chariots and are strong. (Joshua 17:18)

To *cut down* is to remove all obstacles, clear away every hindrance, and make room for the vision to be enlarged. Clear the ground! Clear the trees, and you will begin to see further. As Joshua said to them, *"Its farthest extent shall be yours."* There will be no small place for you. It shall be to the farthest horizon that you can see. No matter what must be cleared off your lot, get on with it. Clear off fear, discouragement, disappointment, lack, poverty, and injustice. Whatever your obstacle is, put the ax to the roots and clear it.

Thus you shall deal with them: you shall destroy their altars, and break down their sacred pillars, and cut down their wooden images, and burn their carved images with fire. (Deuteronomy 7:5)

Drive Out

The attitude of faith will drive out any and all enemies that have set themselves against you. *"For you shall drive out the Canaanites, though they have iron chariots and are strong"* (Joshua 17:18). Drive out all the enemies that have occupied your lot, your present, or your vision. In the spiritual realm, *adversity* signifies *advance*. The more you move into your true, God-given future, the higher you set your goals and the greater the pressure you will experience. Drive out any bad attitudes of unbelief or doubt.

Israel had a vision for their future—a promise that God had given them.

So it shall be, when the LORD your God brings you into the land of which He swore to your fathers, to Abraham, Isaac, and Jacob, to give you large and beautiful cities which you did not build, houses full of all good things, which you did not fill, hewn-out wells which you did not dig, vineyards and olive trees which you did not plant. (Deuteronomy 6:10–11)

I have come down to deliver them out of the hand of the Egyptians, and to bring them up from that land to a good and large land, to a land flowing with milk and honey, to the place of the Canaanites and the Hittites and the Amorites and the Perizzites and the Hivites and the Jebusites. (Exodus 3:8)

Israel shall dwell in safety, the fountain of Jacob alone, in a land of grain and new wine; His heavens shall also drop dew. (Deuteronomy 33:28)

God has also given promises to you, and He is encouraging you to go up, cut down, and drive out all the enemies, because the vision God has for you is to give you much more than you can see or even imagine to be true. It would be right for you to pray the same prayer that Jabez did, right now.

Oh, that You would bless me indeed, and enlarge my territory, that Your hand would be with me, and that You would keep me from evil, that I may not cause pain! (1 Chronicles 4:10)

Take Possession

The promise given to Ephraim and Manasseh, if they would go up, drive out, and cut down, was that God would enable them to possess the vision. They were told to take possession and that they would have all the mountain country to its furthest extent. Taking possession of your future with a faith attitude necessitates taking the faith promise, which requires faith possession. Like Abraham, believe the promise.

> *If you will go up, drive out, and cut down, God will enable you to possess that vision.*

The LORD made a covenant with Abram, saying: "To your descendants I have given this land, from the river of Egypt to the great river, the River Euphrates; the Kenites, the Kenezzites, the Kadmonites, the Hittites, the Perizzites, the Rephaim, the Amorites, the Canaanites, the Girgashites, and the Jebusites." (Genesis 15:18–21)

Believe the promise like Moses did.

I will set your bounds from the Red Sea to the sea, Philistia, and from the desert to the River. For I will deliver the inhabitants of the land into your hand, and you shall drive them out before you.
(Exodus 23:31)

Believe the promise as Joshua did.

The LORD our God spoke to us in Horeb, saying: "You have dwelt long enough at this mountain. Turn and take your journey, and go to the mountains of the Amorites, to all the neighboring places in the plain, in the mountains and in the lowland, in the South and on the seacoast, to the land of the Canaanites and to Lebanon, as far as the great river, the River Euphrates. See, I have set the land before you; go in and possess the land which the LORD swore to your fathers; to Abraham, Isaac, and Jacob; to give to them and their descendants after them."
(Deuteronomy 1:6–8)

Take possession of what God has set before you with an absolute spirit of faith that says, "Yes, Lord, I can." Joshua's response to Ephraim is God's response to us. You have a great inheritance—one that is large enough to meet all your needs. You have great ability to accomplish this vision if you set your will to do it. Do not allow your circumstances to restrict your faith in any way.

Take up Caleb's attitude of faith, which says, *"Let us go up at once and take possession, for we are well able to overcome it"* (Numbers 13:30). God said that Caleb had a different spirit from the rest of the people.

But My servant Caleb, because he has a different spirit in him and has followed Me fully, I will bring into the land where he went, and his descendants shall inherit it. (Numbers 14:24)

Caleb possessed an attitude that followed God fully, undaunted by limitations, fear tactics of the enemy, or fear of what others would say. (See Joshua 14:12–13.) This is the attitude we are to have. This is the attitude of faith that receives the promises of God. God's promises and the attitude of faith to receive them are not limited by age. When Caleb was eighty-five, he had the same spirit of faith and vision to possess the inheritance.

God's promises and our faith in them are also not limited by gender, for the daughters of Ephraim and Manasseh were instrumental in possessing the land, building cities, and fulfilling vision. The daughters of Zelophehad were given an inheritance in Joshua 17:3–4:

> *But Zelophehad the son of Hepher, the son of Gilead, the son of Machir, the son of Manasseh, had no sons, but only daughters. And these are the names of his daughters: Mahlah, Noah, Hoglah, Milcah, and Tirzah. And they came near before Eleazar the priest, before Joshua the son of Nun, and before the rulers, saying, "The LORD commanded Moses to give us an inheritance among our brothers." Therefore, according to the commandment of the LORD, he gave them an inheritance among their father's brothers.*

And in 1 Chronicles 7:24, Sheerah, the daughter of Ephraim, built cities, one of which was constructed at a strategic military location guarding a major pass and a city of refuge. *"His daughter was Sheerah, who built Lower and Upper Beth Horon and Uzzen Sheerah."*

The attitude of faith is the one that Ephraim and Manasseh passed down to their children and to their children's children. It produced many great leaders, such as Joshua, Deborah (see Judges 4:5), Gideon (see Judges 7:24), Samuel (see 1 Samuel 1:1), and Ehud (see Judges 3:27).

The attitude of faith is yours to have and yours to increase. Habakkuk 2:4 says that *"the just shall live by his faith,"* and Romans 1:17 says we should grow *"from faith to faith."* Pray that God will grant you the faith to match the times in which we live and the faith to explore, create, discover, achieve, change, and improve all areas of life. May God grant you a supernatural infusion of faith that drives you forward to capture the future, and may He give you a new spirit of faith to see the unlimited number of possibilities that surround you.

May the attitude of faith grant you the courage to set bold goals that will accomplish great things for God's kingdom. Great faith will enable you to see the invisible, believe the incredible, and receive the impossible. Believe that God will grant you the capacity to reach for the unreasonable. He will never tell you to stoop to guarding only what you have. Increase your faith. Grow. Move forward. Get out of the boat. Walk through new doors.

Conclusion

In the previous chapters, groundwork has been laid for an attitude change in your life. You have been reminded that God has a good destiny for your life—one that is full of hope and joy. You are the only one who can allow that to happen or stop it from happening. It is your choice. If you choose to respond to God in faith, you will see the fulfillment of His promises. But if you choose to hold back in fear, worry, apathy, or laziness, you will continue to live a life of unmet expectations and unlived dreams.

Cultivating Great Faith

You may have started this book with no faith, a little faith, or great faith, but there is always room for faith to grow. In Luke 17:5, *"the apostles said to the Lord, 'Increase our faith.'"* Right now, I want you to pray that prayer. "God, increase my faith." D. L. Moody said,

Some say, "Faith is the gift of God." So is the air; but you have to breathe it. So is bread; but you have to eat it. So is water; but you have to drink it. Some are wanting a miraculous kind of feeling. That is not faith. *"Faith cometh by hearing, and hearing by the word of God"* (Romans 10:17 KJV). That is whence faith comes. It is not for me to sit down and wait for faith to come stealing over me with a strong sensation; but it is for me to take God at His word.[32]

This is the time, this very minute, for you to decide to take God at His word. Choose now. Pray now, "God, increase my faith."

Faith and the Spirit

Faith begins in the spirit. Faith is an attitude of the Holy Spirit, and without the Holy Spirit, you cannot have true faith.

> *But what does it say? "The word is near you, in your mouth and in your heart" (that is, the word of faith which we preach): that if you confess with your mouth the Lord Jesus and believe in your heart that God has raised Him from the dead, you will be saved. For with the heart one believes unto righteousness, and with the mouth confession is made unto salvation.*
> (Romans 10:8–10)

You must be birthed into faith by a spiritual experience—by being born into the Spirit and making Christ your Lord and Savior. If you have not yet made that decision, make it now. Pray the following prayer right now.

I know that I am a sinner and I need forgiveness. I believe that Christ died for my sin. I am willing to turn from my sin. I now invite Jesus Christ to come into my heart and life as my personal Savior. I am willing, by God's grace, to follow and obey Christ as Lord of my life.

Faith and the Mind

Faith is nurtured by the proper functioning of the mind. The spirit of faith is assimilated into the mind and merged with the Word of God residing in the mind, creating a chemistry of growing faith. Begin today to discipline your mind in right thinking—thinking that is in agreement with the Word of God.

Romans 12:2 commands you to *"be transformed by the renewing of your mind, that you may prove what is that good and acceptable and perfect will of God."* Memorize this Scripture and, in accordance with Psalm 1:2, meditate on it both day and night until your thoughts begin to align with God's thoughts.

Faith and the Will

Faith is transformed into action through the will. Your will is the *discipline* part of faith—your ability to continue forward in spite of opposition. Begin to speak the Word instead of giving voice to your fears. Speak the memorized Word; declare the promises of God.

In the Greek, to *confess* means "to say the same thing as," so begin confessing the Word of God, saying the same things that God is saying. Your emotions may not agree, but do not allow your emotions to rule or reign over you. Align your will with God's will and allow His Spirit to direct your words, thoughts, and actions. Say yes to God with the words that you speak, say yes to God with the thoughts you allow yourself to think, and say yes to God with your actions.

Choose the Attitude of Faith

Today is the day. This is your *kairos* time. You have come to the end of this book and the beginning of your new life story. What will you write into your future? The pen is in your hand, and you must write. Will you write of the goodness of God? Will you write of the promises of God? God made the promises. God gave the dream. Now, you must decide to choose the attitude of faith. You must choose to say yes to the power of God in your life.

Endnotes

1. The first four paragraphs of this chapter are paraphrased from "Teaching an old dog new tricks" (http://www.elmwoodchurch. ca/archive.php?id=105) by Rev. Kevin Steeper of Elmwood Avenue Presbyterian Church in London, Ontario, 12 March 2006. Used by permission.

2. George Bernard Shaw, quoted by Richard Burton, *Little Essays in Literature and Life* (New York: The Century Company, 1914), 94–95.

3. Amy Carmichael, quoted by V. Raymond Edman, *They Found the Secret: 20 Transformed Lives That Reveal a Touch of Eternity* (Grand Rapids, MI: Zondervan, 1984), 50.

4. William Carey, quoted by Henry Wheeler Robinson and Ernest Alexander Payne, *British Baptists: An Original Anthology* (Manchester, NH: Ayer Publishing, 1980), 114.

5. Langston Hughes, *The Collected Works of Langston Hughes* (Columbia, MO: University of Missouri Press, 2001), 409.

6. Allen Gardiner, quoted by Arthur Tappan Pierson and Andrew Thomson, *The New Acts of the Apostles: Or the Marvels of Modern Missions* (New York: Baker and Taylor, 1894), 112.

7. Elizabeth McEwen Shields, *As the Day Begins* (Richmond: John Knox Press, 1944).

8. Bernard de Clairvaux, *Saint Bernard, Abbot of Clairvaux: selections from his letters, meditations, sermons, hymns, and other writings*, trans. Horatio Grimley (New York: Cambridge University Press, 1910), 194.

9. Andrew Murray, *Andrew Murray Devotional: A 365-Day Devotional* (New Kensington, PA: Whitaker House, 2006), 15 (January 4).

10. Brother Lawrence, *The Practice of the Presence of God* (New Kensington, PA: Whitaker House, 1982), 68.

11. A. W. Tozer, *The Pursuit of God* (Radford, VA: Wilder Publications, 2008), 9.

12. Andrew Murray, *Daily Secrets of Christian Living: A Daily Devotional*, comp. Al Bryant (Grand Rapids, MI: Kregel Publications, 1996), December 19.

13. Henri J. M. Nouwen, *Making All Things New: An Invitation to the Spiritual Life* (New York: HarperCollins, 1981), 66.

14. William Arthur Ward, quoted by Anthony Zeiss, *Build Your Own Ladder: 4 Secrets to Making Your Career Dreams Come True* (Nashville: Thomas Nelson, 2006), 48.

15. Henry David Thoreau, *Walden* (New York: T. Y. Crowell & Co., 1910), 8.

16. Les and Leslie Parrott, *Relationships: How to Make Bad Relationships Better and Good Relationships Great* (Grand Rapids, MI: Zondervan, 2002), 169–170.

17. Bill Bright, *God: Discover His Character* (Orlando, FL: New Life Publications, 1999), 43–44. Used by permission of Bright Media Foundation and Campus Crusade for Christ. © 1999–2009 Bright Media Foundation, written by Bill Bright. All rights reserved. No part of this book may be reproduced, stored in a retrieval system, or transmitted in any form or by any means, except in articles or reviews, without permission in writing from the publisher.

18. Bright, *God*, 65.

19. Charles W. Colson, *Loving God* (Grand Rapids, MI: Zondervan, 2006), 25.

20. Hudson Taylor, quoted by Thomas E. Stephens, "One of Hudson Taylor's Helpers," in *Good News for Russia: A Series of Addresses,*

ed. Jesse Wendell Brooks (Chicago: The Bible Institute Colportage Association [Moody Press], 1918), 32.

21. C. S. Lewis, *The Weight of Glory* (New York: HarperOne, 2001), 26.

22. Augustine, quoted by Rudolf John Harvey, The *Metaphysical Relation between Person and Liberty* (Washington, D.C.: Catholic University of America Press, 1942), 140.

23. Craig Boldman and Peter Matthews, *Every Excuse in the Book: 714 Ways to Say "It's Not My Fault!"* (Kansas City, MO: Andrews McMeel Publishing, 1998).

24. Andy Serwer, "Larry Page on how to change the world," *Fortune Magazine* (May 1, 2008), http://money.cnn.com/2008/04/29/magazines/fortune/larry_page_change_the_world.fortune/.

25. Eleanor Roosevelt, *You Learn by Living: Eleven Keys for a More Fulfilling Life* (Louisville, KY: Westminster John Knox Press, 1983), 29–20.

26. Frederick F. Bruce, quoted by Gary S. Greig and Kevin N. Springer, eds., *The Kingdom and the Power: Are Healing and the Spiritual Gifts Used by Jesus and the Early Church Meant for the Church Today? A Biblical Look at How to Bring the Gospel to the World with Power* (Ventura, CA: Regal Books, 1993), 24.

27. Alan Richardson, quoted by Greig and Springer, *The Kingdom and the Power*, 25.

28. H. Van der Loos, quoted by Greig and Springer, *The Kingdom and the Power*, 26.

29. Augustine, *The City of God: A New Translation*, vol. 24 (Books 17–22), trans. Gerald G. Walsh (Fathers of the Church, 1954), Book 22, ch. 8, pg. 445.

30. Justin Martyr, *Saint Justin Martyr: The First Apology, the Second Apology, Dialogue with Trypho, Exhortation to the Greeks, Discourse to the Greeks, the Monarchy, Or the Rule of God*, trans. Thomas B. Falls (Washington, D.C.: Catholic University of America Press, 1965), 125–126.

31. *Hudson Taylor's Choice Sayings: A Compilation from His Writings and Addresses* (London: China Inland Mission, n.d.), 13.

32. Dwight Lyman Moody, *The Way to God* (New York: Cosimo Classics, 2005), 53.